Cloud Analytics wi
Cloud Platform

An end-to-end guide to processing and analyzing big data
using Google Cloud Platform

Sanket Thodge

BIRMINGHAM - MUMBAI

Cloud Analytics with Google Cloud Platform

Commissioning Editor: Amey Varangaonkar
Acquisition Editor: Viraj Madhav
Content Development Editor: Varun Sony
Technical Editor: Dinesh Chaudhary
Copy Editor: Safis Editing
Project Coordinator: Manthan Patel
Proofreader: Safis Editing
Indexer: Aishwarya Gangawane
Graphics: Tania Dutta
Production Coordinator: Aparna Bhagat

First published: April 2018

Production reference: 1060418

Published by Packt Publishing Ltd.
Livery Place
35 Livery Street
Birmingham
B3 2PB, UK.

ISBN 978-1-78883-968-6

www.packtpub.com

`mapt.io`

Mapt is an online digital library that gives you full access to over 5,000 books and videos, as well as industry leading tools to help you plan your personal development and advance your career. For more information, please visit our website.

Why subscribe?

- Spend less time learning and more time coding with practical eBooks and Videos from over 4,000 industry professionals

- Improve your learning with Skill Plans built especially for you

- Get a free eBook or video every month

- Mapt is fully searchable

- Copy and paste, print, and bookmark content

PacktPub.com

Did you know that Packt offers eBook versions of every book published, with PDF and ePub files available? You can upgrade to the eBook version at `www.PacktPub.com` and as a print book customer, you are entitled to a discount on the eBook copy. Get in touch with us at `service@packtpub.com` for more details.

At `www.PacktPub.com`, you can also read a collection of free technical articles, sign up for a range of free newsletters, and receive exclusive discounts and offers on Packt books and eBooks.

Foreword

Over last three decades, the computing industry is moving in a definite direction. Big and centralized systems such as mainframes have been replaced by small virtual systems in cloud.

Instead of using computer hardware and software within a firm's own network or data-center (or an individual's laptop), the same computing power is available as a service and these services are offered by specialist companies. This computing power can be accessed over the internet seamlessly.

Personal devices such as tablets, PCs, and mobiles generate tens of trillions of data points. If someone can analyze such a volume of data then this offers countless possibilities to use such a data for larger good of the society which include ease in governance or businesses. Businesses make use of it for commercial gains. Cloud is the best and the most economical platform to introspect and comprehend such large volumes of data we all generate every minute these days.

However, analyzing such a large volume of data requires a huge cache of computing power which is expensive and capital intensive. One of the quick solutions is to utilize the on-demand and managed computing services in cloud which can be scaled within no time, put to use and discarded at the end of specific analysis. In fact, most cloud vendors offer specialized services which can be better described as analytics as a service.

It is not easy to foray into this technical domain. It involves learning the cloud, internals of cloud, hardware, software, virtualization and hundreds of services each cloud vendor offers.

This book simplifies complex topics such as cloud, types of cloud, their offerings and compares major cloud platforms such as Amazon AWS, Microsoft Azure and Google GCP for quick learning. Chapters in the book are dedicated to Google Cloud Platform specifically for analytics purpose and describes in great detail how to use the Google platform for such analytics.

This book not only demonstrates a detailed understanding of complex suite of tools offered by GCP for analytics, but also describes similar tools from other cloud vendors. This book dedicates many chapters to how to move data to GCP, ingest, analyze, visualize, and is inclusive of the use of artificial intelligence and machine learning techniques. Most importantly, the theoretical description is complemented by detailed discussion of use cases. Besides analytics, this book also describes the value of cloud certification and the required know-how for GCP Architect certification.

-Anand Vemula

Expert in AWS with 19 years of experience in software engineering and is the Vice President for world's leading bank firm.

Contributors

About the author

Sanket Thodge is an entrepreneur by profession based out of Pune, India. He started his journey in the service industry, but soon incorporated startup with the name Pi R Square Digital Solutions Pvt. Ltd. With expertise in Hadoop Developer, he explored Cloud, IoT, Machine Learning, and Blockchain. He has also applied for a patent in IoT and has worked with numerous startups and multinationals in providing consultancy, architecture building, development, and corporate training across the globe.

About the reviewers

Rajeev Goel has over 24 years of experience as a software architect in project management, software development, and presales. He has worked on various cloud computing and big data technologies. He received his BE (electronics) from Shivaji University. He is currently a freelance trainer and consultant. His previous experience includes big names in the IT industry and clients in construction, telecoms, manufacturing/automobile, finance, and the public sector.

Dr. M Varaprasad Rao is a professor in the department of computer science at the CMR technical campus. He has a teaching experience of over 16 years, both in academia and industry. He is involved in teaching courses at both UG and PG levels, including curriculum development. His research interests include data mining, security, cloud, and analytics. He was a BoS member. He has contributed 25 papers, 4 book chapters to IGI Global, and has 3 patents. He is a lifetime member of CSI, ISTE, and IAEng.

Rakesh Porwad has 7.4 years of overall IT Experience, of which 3.5 years of experience is in Hadoop, spark, and cloud technology and the rest of experience in Java technology. He is currently working with Capgemini as a Spark developer. He has completed BE in electronics and telecommunication streams in 2010. He has been a winner of the project competition organized at IIT Bombay TechFest. He has participated in International conferences. He is also a winner of Google Cloud Platform Hackthon organized intercompany.

Saket Karnik, a name with rigorous 19 years dedication to technology is now known in the enterprise circle for dependable Microsoft Azure deep-dive sessions. With Microsoft certifications such as MCT, MCTS, and MCP, his training and consulting expertise ranges from Azure to Oracle frameworks. He has also authored the Azure IoT curriculum for Microsoft Campus Connect Program, Hyderabad. He will soon be delivering his 555th corporate session for yet another batch of enthusiastic laterals.

Packt is searching for authors like you

If you're interested in becoming an author for Packt, please visit authors.packtpub.com and apply today. We have worked with thousands of developers and tech professionals, just like you, to help them share their insight with the global tech community. You can make a general application, apply for a specific hot topic that we are recruiting an author for, or submit your own idea.

Table of Contents

Preface

With the ongoing data explosion, more and more organizations all over the world are slowly migrating their infrastructure to the cloud. These cloud platforms also provide distinct analytics services to help you get faster insights from your data.

This book will give you an introduction to the concept of analytics on the cloud and the different cloud services popularly used for processing and analyzing data. If you're planning to adopt the cloud analytics model for your business, this book will help you in understanding the design and business considerations to keep in mind, and choose the best tools and alternatives for analytics based on your requirements. The chapters in this book will take you through the 70+ services available on the **Google Cloud Platform** (**GCP**) and their implementation for practical purposes. From ingestion to processing your data, this book contains best practices on choosing right services required to build an end-to-end analytics pipeline on the cloud by leveraging popular concepts such as machine learning and deep learning.

This book is also covering GCP certification aspect and a chapter is dedicated to give you a boost start in GCP certification preparation. Also, readers who have worked on AWS and Azure can refer to the appendix if they are willing to understand which are the different services in GCP, AWS, and Azure provisioning the same purpose.

By the end of this book, you will have a better understanding of cloud analytics as a concept as well as a practical know-how of its implementation.

Who this book is for

This book is targeted at CIOs, CTOs, and even analytics professionals looking for various alternatives to implement their analytics pipeline on the cloud. Data professionals looking to get started with cloud-based analytics will also find this book useful. Some basic exposure to cloud platforms such as GCP will be helpful, but it is not mandatory.

Book focuses on major aspects of each tool - utility, architecture, use cases, pricing, and right fit. But for you to get the complete understanding of each tool we have provided links to YouTube videos which will help you with the practical aspects of the services in GCP.

What this book covers

Chapter 1, *Introducing Cloud Analytics,* discusses the traditional way that companies prefer to build their on-premise architecture for analytics. This will majorly discuss the enterprises' approach towards the analytics engine how they handle/process/report data. It will also give an introduction to analytics and data science concepts. And the top cloud vendors who provides it. This chapter will also give a brief overview of cloud computing.

Chapter 2, *Design and Business Considerations,* talks more about the design and architecture of the cloud. Before moving to the cloud, do we need to consider on-premise hardware or should we consider moving it straight away? What are the prerequisites before migrating to the cloud? And the best practices to follow for migration. Topics like these will be covered.

Chapter 3, *GCP 10,000 Feet Above – A High-Level Understanding of GCP,* explains all the analytics tools such as Datastore, BigTable, BigQuery, Cloud SQL, machine learning, IoT, Pub/Sub, and many more in detail.

Here we are covering all the services in GCP and appending them with top features, pricing, use cases of all the services.

Chapter 4, *Ingestion and Storing – Bring the Data and Capture It,* dives into the major services involving ingestion and storing. We have multiple options associated with ingestion and storage. We will be discussing about eight major services which can help us with ingestion and storage. We have videos for each of the services.

There will be a few cloud use cases from the industry about the purpose of each tool.

Chapter 5, *Processing and Visualizing – Close Encounter, Squeeze the Data and Make It Work,* discusses the processing tools and machine learning APIs that are available with GCP. GCP has extensive tools for processing data. For processing, we have Cloud Dataproc (Hadoop and Spark). BigQuery, Cloud SQL, and more will be covered. We have videos for each of the services.

Chapter 6, *Machine Learning, Deep Learning, and AI on GCP,* talks predominantly about artificial intelligence and machine learning. In the beginning of the chapter, we will understand what artificial intelligence is, and later, we will understand what machine learning is. We have videos for most of the services.

Chapter 7, *Guidance on Google Cloud Platform Certification,* focuses mainly on GCP certification with respect to cloud architects and data engineers. Along with that, it will also have some dummy/sample questions from certification.

Chapter 8, *Business Use Cases*, includes examples from multiple sectors sectors. They will help the reader get a more precise understanding of the cloud and how they are used. We have three use cases - they talk about the problem statement, different approach towards each problem, solution to each, architecture, and list of services required.

Chapter 9, *Introduction to AWS and Azure*, covers the major tools in AWS and Azure about data science and analytics. Most of the tools will be closely related to data science. The aim of this chapter will be relating the GCP tools with AWS and Azure. For example, we have cloud storage in GCP, and similarly we have S3 in AWS and Blob Storage in Azure.

To get the most out of this book

1. Basic exposure to cloud platforms such as GCP will be helpful but is not mandatory.
2. Good understanding of any development language
3. SQL and Unix skills required in few of the services

Download the color images

We also provide a PDF file that has color images of the screenshots/diagrams used in this book. You can download it here:
http://www.packtpub.com/sites/default/files/downloads/CloudAnalyticswithGoogleC loudPlatform_ColorImages.pdf.

Conventions used

There are a number of text conventions used throughout this book.

CodeInText: Indicates code words in text, database table names, folder names, filenames, file extensions, pathnames, dummy URLs, user input, and Twitter handles. Here is an example: "Mount the downloaded WebStorm-10*.dmg disk image file as another disk in your system."

Bold: Indicates a new term, an important word, or words that you see onscreen. For example, words in menus or dialog boxes appear in the text like this. Here is an example: "Select **System info** from the **Administration** panel."

Warnings or important notes appear like this.

 Tips and tricks appear like this.

Get in touch

Feedback from our readers is always welcome.

General feedback: Email feedback@packtpub.com and mention the book title in the subject of your message. If you have questions about any aspect of this book, please email us at questions@packtpub.com.

Errata: Although we have taken every care to ensure the accuracy of our content, mistakes do happen. If you have found a mistake in this book, we would be grateful if you would report this to us. Please visit www.packtpub.com/submit-errata, selecting your book, clicking on the Errata Submission Form link, and entering the details.

Piracy: If you come across any illegal copies of our works in any form on the Internet, we would be grateful if you would provide us with the location address or website name. Please contact us at copyright@packtpub.com with a link to the material.

If you are interested in becoming an author: If there is a topic that you have expertise in and you are interested in either writing or contributing to a book, please visit authors.packtpub.com.

Reviews

Please leave a review. Once you have read and used this book, why not leave a review on the site that you purchased it from? Potential readers can then see and use your unbiased opinion to make purchase decisions, we at Packt can understand what you think about our products, and our authors can see your feedback on their book. Thank you!

For more information about Packt, please visit packtpub.com.

Introducing Cloud Analytics 1

In this chapter, we are going to learn the important aspects of cloud analytics. We are going to build a platform to get a better understanding of **Google Cloud Platform** (**GCP**) and its tools. This chapter will help you in understanding the purpose of GCP, the motto behind different tools and services that we have on the platform. But while we are learning about cloud analytics, cloud computing and analytics are also very important topics to cover. Thereafter, we are also going to learn about the major benefits of having cloud computing and having analytics in production. These topics will be covered in a very simple way.

As we go ahead in the chapter, we will also learn about the analytics part associated with the cloud. The cloud is not only about using the infrastructure of vendors, but along with that we also need to use our data on the cloud appropriately. Some cloud vendors do have their own tools over cloud to use this data, and a few are reliant on other cloud vendors to provide the same service. Once we are clear on these topics, we will learn the merging of cloud computing and analytics and will give birth to cloud analytics. The role of cloud analytics in the industry will be studied and what benefit it has over traditional systems.

We will cover the following topics in this chapter:

- What is cloud computing?
- Major benefits of cloud computing
- Cloud computing deployment models
- Types of cloud computing services
- How PaaS, IaaS, and SaaS are separated at service level
- Emerging cloud technologies and services
- Cloud computing security
- A brief history of cloud computing

- Risk and challenges with cloud
- What is cloud analytics?
- 10 major cloud vendors in the world

What is cloud computing?

I don't need a hard disk in my computer if I can get to the server faster, simply carrying around these non-connected computers is byzantine by comparison.
- Steve Jobs, Co-founder, CEO, and Chairman of Apple Inc.

This quote is very significant, not because it's by Steve Jobs, but the fact that it was adopted and accepted by him—that yes, cloud holds a huge value to him and eventually to his company.

We have been listening, reading, and thinking about cloud computing—but what exactly is it? Is it a supercomputer? Or is it software? Or is the supercomputer sent to the cloud at the height of 35,000 feet for better cooling? How well do we know what cloud is? And how well do we know what cloud computing is? Have you ever given a thought on the fact of what is cloud computing? Okay, so you may know what cloud computing is, but have you heard of Cloud Analytics?

We are going to discuss the same things in this chapter. So, if you consider yourself very naive in the field of cloud, don't bother about that, because every master was once a student. Before understanding cloud analytics, we have to break down the topic bit by bit. Cloud analytics is a combination of cloud computing and analytics.

To date, the industry has been focusing on cloud computing and analytics as separate entities. But now, as we are evolving and adopting new technologies at a faster rate, cloud analytics will the new wave. In the traditional world, organizations were building their own infrastructure. This framework/infrastructure included buying a huge number of servers, network wires, and cooling mechanisms, and then fitting them together.

Along with this came the headache of maintaining it with huge infrastructure and human costs. And upgrading the outdated hardware was a different challenge altogether.

So, before learning about cloud analytics and taking a deep dive, we will understand what cloud computing is and what analytics is.

Firms are assisted by the exponential development of cloud analytics to use a compute resource, such as a **virtual machine (VM)**—the same way we use electricity.

Major benefits of cloud computing

Cloud computing offers amazing benefits for users, such as:

- **Self-service provisioning infrastructure**: Customers can compute resources for any requirement. This removes the traditional need for IT administrators / IT architects to provision and handle compute resources.

- **Flexibility to scale up and down**: Enterprises can scale up and down as computing needs increase or decrease as demand varies. Due to this you are not required to do any massive investments in local infrastructure, which may remain active or inactive as per requirement.

- **Workload resilience**: Many times, superfluous resources are reserved for cloud service to keep the storage seamless across the globe.

- **Pay per resource use**: To ensure people pay only for the cloud computing resource they expend, calculations are done at the absolute minuscule level. No overcharging, and bills under control.

- **Flexibility to migrate**: Enterprises can migrate certain resources to or from the cloud—or to different cloud vendors—as desired or automatically for better cost savings or better performance or to use new services as they emerge.

- **Disaster readiness**: Against the previous understanding that we need to invest in heavy hardware to have backup recovery, to avoid global outage we need global servers, which are now eliminated due to the presence of cloud platforms.

- **Automatic upgrades, working anywhere, and increased collaboration**: With cloud we are reduced with the hassle of upgrading the hardware and software. The only thing that you should be concerned about is your product and service. With cloud you also get an opportunity to work independently of the infrastructure, all you need is a system to connect to cloud and the internet. Thus, when you are not worried about upgradation and infrastructure you can collaborate with anyone and from anywhere.

- **And the best part is, security**: Cloud platforms provide you with the best security standards available in the world. Your code is secured, your data is secured, and your customer identity is secured. All you need to worry about is your product and how to build it.

Now that we have understood the basics of cloud computing and their benefits, let's see what types of cloud deployments we can have in enterprises.

Cloud computing deployment models

Cloud computing as much about learning the architecture as it is about the different deployment options that we have. We need to know the different ways our cloud infrastructure can be kept open to the world and do we want to restrict it. There are three ways of cloud computing and its deployment:

- Private cloud
- Public cloud
- Hybrid cloud

Private cloud

Private cloud services are built specifically when companies want to hold everything to them. It provides the users with customization in choosing hardware, in all the software options, and storage options. This typically works as a central data center to the internal end users. This model reduces the dependencies on external vendors. Enterprise users accessing this cloud may or may not be billed for utilizing the services.

Private cloud changes how an enterprise decides the architecture of the cloud and how they are going to apply it in their infrastructure. Administration of a private cloud environment can be carried by internal or outsourced staff.

Common private cloud technologies and vendors include the following:

- VMware: https://cloud.vmware.com
- OpenStack: https://www.openstack.org
- Citrix: https://www.citrix.co.in/products/citrix-cloud
- CloudStack: https://cloudstack.apache.org
- Go Grid: https://www.datapipe.com/gogrid

With a private cloud, the same organization is showing itself as the cloud consumer as well as the cloud provider, as the infrastructure is built by them and the consumers are also from the same enterprise. But in order to differentiate these roles, *a separate organizational department typically assumes the responsibility for provisioning the cloud and therefore assumes the cloud provider role, whereas the departments requiring access to this established private cloud take the role of the cloud consumer:*

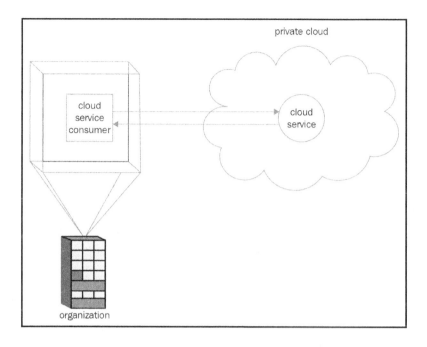

Public cloud

In a public cloud deployment model, third-party cloud service provider often provide the cloud service over the internet . Public cloud services are sold with respect to demand and by a minute or hour basis. But if you want, you can go for a long term commitment for up to five years in some cases, such as renting a virtual machine. In the case of renting a virtual machine, the customers pay for the duration, storage, or bandwidth that they consume (this might vary from vendor to vendor).

Major public cloud service providers include:

- Google Cloud Platform: https://cloud.google.com
- Amazon Web Services: https://aws.amazon.com
- IBM: https://www.ibm.com/cloud
- Microsoft Azure: https://azure.microsoft.com
- Rackspace: https://www.rackspace.com/cloud

The architecture of a public cloud will typically go as follows:

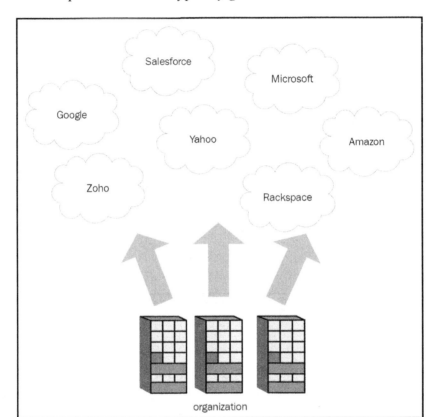

Hybrid cloud

The next and the last cloud deployment type is the **hybrid cloud**. A hybrid cloud is an amalgamation of public cloud services (GCP, AWS, Azure likes) and an on-premises private cloud (built by respective enterprise). Both on-premise and public have their roles here. On-premise are more for mission-critical applications, whereas public cloud manage spikes in demand. Automation is enabled between both the environment.

The following figure shows the architecture of a hybrid cloud:

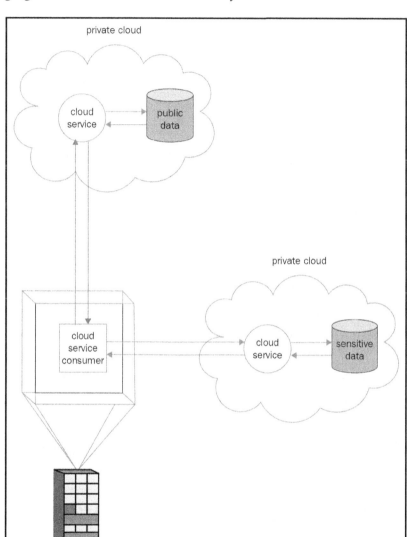

The major benefit of a hybrid cloud is to create a uniquely unified, superbly automated, and insanely scalable environment that takes the benefit of everything a public cloud infrastructure has to offer, while still maintaining control over mission-critical vital data.

Some common hybrid cloud examples include:

- **Hitachi hybrid cloud:** `https://www.hitachivantara.com/en-us/solutions/hybrid-cloud.html`
- **Rackspace:** `https://www.rackspace.com/en-in/cloud/hybrid`
- **IBM:** `https://www.ibm.com/it-infrastructure/z/capabilities/hybrid-cloud`
- **AWS:** `https://aws.amazon.com/enterprise/hybrid`

Differences between the private cloud, hybrid cloud, and public cloud models

The following tables summarizes the differences between the three cloud deployment models:

	Private	Hybrid	Public
Definition	A cloud computing model in which enterprises uses its own proprietary software and hardware. And this is specifically limited to its own data centre. Servers, cooling system, and storage - everything belongs to the company.	This model includes a mixture of private and public cloud. It has a few components on-premises, private cloud and it will also be connected to other services on public cloud with perfect orchestration.	Here, we have a complete third-part or a company that lets us use their infrastructure for a given period of time. This is a pay-as-you-use model. General public can access their infrastructure and no in-house servers are required to be maintained.
Characteristics	• Single-tenant architecture • On-premises hardware • Direct control of the hardware	• Cloud bursting capacities • Advantages of both public and private cloud • Freedom to choose services from multiple vendors	• Pay-per use model • Multi-tenant model
Vendors	HPE, VMWare, Microsoft, OpenStack	Combination of public and private	Google Cloud Platform, Amazon Web Services, Microsoft Azure

Types of cloud computing services

Cloud computing has upgraded to a huge extent in recent times, and it has been divided into three major service categories:

- **Infrastructure as a Service (IaaS)**
- **Platform as a Service (PaaS)**
- **Software as a Service (SaaS)**

We will discuss each of these instances in the following sections.

Infrastructure as a Service

Infrastructure as a Service often provides the infrastructure such as servers, virtual machines, networks, operating system, storage, and much more on a pay-as-you-use basis. IaaS providers offer VM from small to extra-large machines.

The IaaS gives you complete freedom while choosing the instance type as per your requirements:

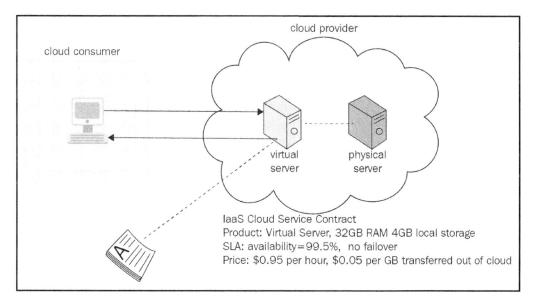

Common cloud vendors providing the IaaS services are:

- Google Cloud Platform
- Amazon Web Services
- IBM
- HP Public Cloud

PaaS

The PaaS model is similar to IaaS, but it also provides the additional tools such as database management system, business intelligence services, and so on. The following figure illustrates the architecture of the PaaS model:

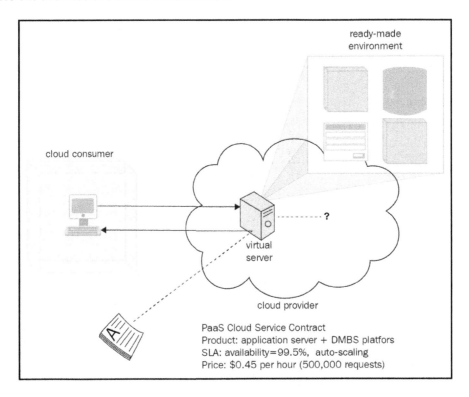

Cloud platforms providing PaaS services are as follows:

- Windows Azure
- Google App Engine
- Cloud Foundry
- Amazon Web Services

SaaS

Software as a Service (SaaS) makes the users connect to the products through the internet (or sometimes also help them build in-house as a private cloud solution) on a subscription basis model.

Below image shows the basic architecture of SaaS model.

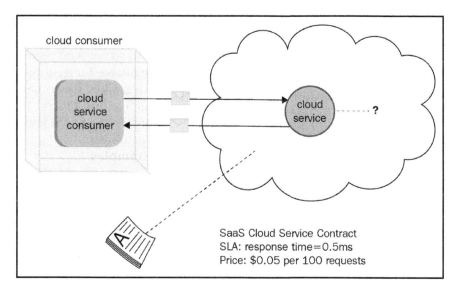

Some cloud vendors providing SaaS are:

- Google Application
- Salesforce
- Zoho
- Microsoft Office 365

Differences between SaaS, PaaS, and IaaS

The major differences between these models can be summarized to a table as follows:

Software as a Service (SaaS)	Platform as a Service (PaaS)	Infrastructure as a Service (IaaS)
Software as a service is a model in which a third-party provider hosts multiple applications and lets customers use them over the internet. SaaS is a very useful pay-as-you-use model. **Examples:** Salesforce, NetSuite	This is a model in which a third-party provider application development platform and services built on its own infrastructure. Again these tools are made available to customers over the internet. **Examples:** Google App Engine, AWS Lambda	In IaaS, a third-party application provides servers, storage, compute resources, and so on. And then makes it available for customers for their utilization. Customers can use IaaS to build their own PaaS and SaaS service for their customers. **Examples:** Google Cloud Compute, Amazon S3

How PaaS, IaaS, and SaaS are separated at service level

In this section, we are going to learn about how we can separate IaaS, PaaS, and SaaS at the service level:

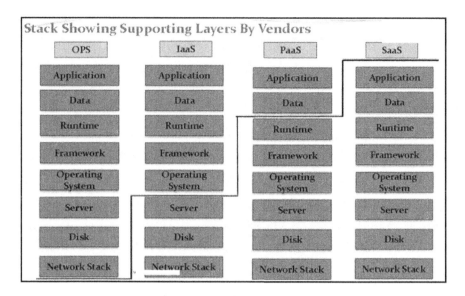

As the previous diagram suggests, we have the first column as OPS, which stands for operations. That means the bare minimum requirement for any typical server. When we are going with a server to buy, we should consider the preceding features before buying.

It includes Application, Data, Runtime, Framework, Operating System, Server, Disk, and Network Stack.

When we move to cloud and decide to go with IaaS—in this case we are not bothered about server, disk, and network stack. Thus, the headache of handling hardware part is no more with us. That's why it is called Infrastructure as a Service.

Now if we think of PaaS, we should not be worried about runtime, framework, and operating system along with the components in IaaS. Things that we need to focus on are only application and data.

And the last deployment model is SaaS—Software as a Service. In this model we are not concerned about literally anything. The only thing that we need to work on is the code and just a look at the bill. It's that simple!

Emerging cloud technologies and services

With cloud analytics we are having many emerging cloud technologies and services which were not present earlier. We will be discussing about few of them below:

- **Serverless:** With serverless computing, developers are only responsible for the code. Developers has to upload code to the cloud and cloud vendor will load and execute it. In responses to different events. These events then triggers in backend some defined functions to perform the given task. Customer in turn pay only for the resources used to run those functions. AWS Lambda, Google Cloud Functions, and Azure Functions are examples of serverless computing services that we have in major cloud vendors.
- **Artificial Intelligence and Machine Learning:** Other major cloud technology is artificial intelligence and machine learning. AI and ML are creating waves in cloud vendors as well. Every cloud vendor is trying to integrate as many as AI, ML and Deep Learning services as possible. They are also providing services to build custom models. Google Cloud Machine Learning Engine and Google Cloud Speech API are services available in Google Cloud Platform, whereas in AWS we have Amazon Machine Learning, and AWS has Rekognition.
- **BigData and Analytics:** This is not really an emerging technology, but lot of innovation is taking place here. Highly available RDBMS are being introduced, petabyte scale NoSQL databases are in place now, and many other aspects like this are shaping the paradigm of BigData and Analytics. Cloud providers now have a good number of big data services, including **Google BigQuery** for large-scale data warehousing and **Amazon Web Services Elastic MapReduce** and **Microsoft Azure Data Lake Analytics** for processing huge datasets, be it structured or unstructured.

Different ways to secure the cloud

Now, as we have seen the concerns and threats on cloud, let us now look at the different features provided by the cloud vendors to secure the cloud data storage:

- **Secure access**: Secure Access is going to help the customer secure access with a username and password, or security keys on a few occasions.
- **Built-in firewalls**: Cloud platform also provides built-in firewalls. They not only protect your services with the DoS attack by allowing certain IP address, but can also keep certain ports open.

- **Unique user**: You can also create your own unique user using an IAM tool, which is available for free by most cloud vendors.
- **Multi factor authentication**: Multi factor Authentication (MFA) is another major leap in providing security. You can use Google's virtual MFA app **Authenticator** to safeguard your systems.
- **Private Subnet**: If you want you can also create your private Subnet and can have more and better control over your network.
- **Encrypted data storage**: You can also encrypt your data at rest, which means you can encrypt the data that you have in the cloud. No one in the world will be able to read this data without having an awareness of the decryption method.
- **Dedicated connection option**: This is typically a special service in which the cloud vendor will give you access to the edge node and thus the data that you are uploading will bypass the normal internet method to reach a cloud vendor's data center, but it will be sent directly to the cloud vendor.

These features makes the cloud vendors more robust, strong, and very secure!

Risks and challenges with the cloud

Now that we have discussed what cloud offerings we have, let's see the challenges that we might have to face:

- **Increased Security Vulnerabilities**: When we plan to adopt cloud services in our architecture trust plays a huge role. Because when data is with us, it is under our complete control. We control the services accessing the data, along with privileges, encryption, and many other things. But when it comes to moving services to cloud its often a very tough call as we are giving all our data and control to cloud. And most times the encryption and security plays a major hindrance while adopting cloud. Thus, security can be a major topic to discuss when it comes to risks involved in cloud.

- **Reduced operational governance control**: As we know by now our infrastructure is shared by other customers of the cloud vendor as well, it brings some constraints to handling the governance aspect for enterprises. You literally lose control over data. And internet is the only connectivity between enterprise and cloud - one more hurdle while taking care of governance. The following figure illustrates this:

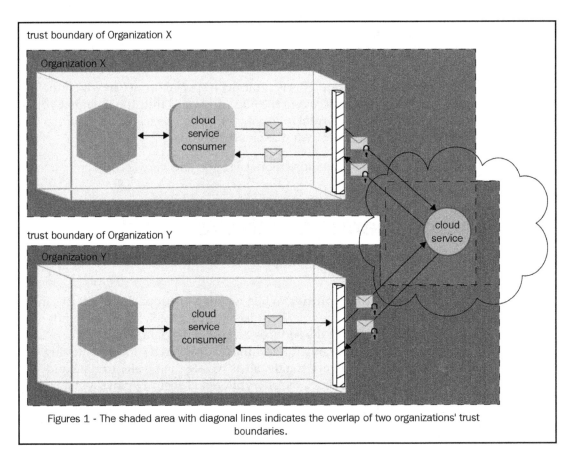

Figures 1 - The shaded area with diagonal lines indicates the overlap of two organizations' trust boundaries.

- **Limited portability between cloud providers:** Given we have many cloud vendors now and no industry standards in terms of technology or communication between services it becomes very difficult for customers to switch from one cloud provider to another. Most of the services are custom built by cloud providers, thus limited portability. The following figure shows two different cloud providers and the features they support for a cloud consumer:

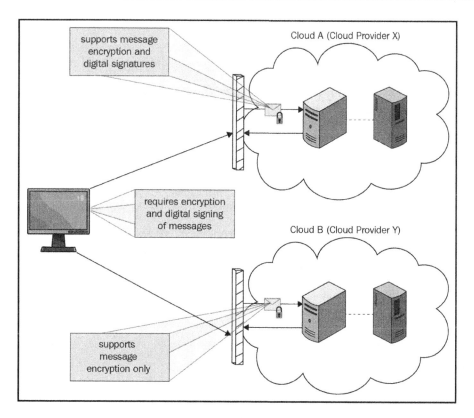

- **Multi-Regional regulatory and legal issues:** When cloud vendor start establishing their data centers across globe the priority is often given to electricity prices, ease of starting data centre, geographical region, potential customers coming from same region and many more. Thus, due to this many time enterprises don't have grasp over the flow of data. But it is taken very seriously by many enterprises and governments. Many countries have a common policy of making companies retain data of the their citizens in the same country. Sometimes, this can become a cause of companies not adopting cloud based solutions.

Now that we understood risk and challenges of cloud computing let's try and understand about cloud analytics.

What is cloud analytics?

Now that we know what cloud computing is, let's get started with cloud analytics.

When we talk about cloud analytics we need to understand that what falls under cloud analytics - is that only analytics or data cleaning as well? Is service of showing graphs and report part of cloud analytics? Or not? And do we need to have just one feature among all to be called as a cloud analytics service enabled cloud or we need all of them? Let's have a look on it.

Under cloud analytics we have tools of the data analytics, data processing, and data manipulating. We often go for a subscription based or pay-as-you-go model.

Then we have a definition from Gartner. They says we have six key elements of analytics to define. And these six elements will decide if a cloud vendor is providing cloud analytics or not. The six elements are given below:

- Data models
- Processing applications
- Analytic models
- Computing power
- Sharing or storage of results
- Data sources

If the cloud vendor is having service for serving all the above purpose, then we can say given cloud vendor has cloud analytics services - and now most of the cloud vendor has it.

Examples of cloud analytics products and services include hosted data warehouses, **Software-as-a-Service Business Intelligence (SaaS BI)**, cloud-based social media analytics, or cloud based NoSQL databases.

So far we have discussed the major aspects of what cloud computing and cloud analytics is and the major differences between IaaS and PaaS. Now we are going to discuss the different cloud vendors that we have in the market.

10 major cloud vendors in the world

Now that we have discussed cloud services and properties, let us take a glance on the major 10 cloud vendors in the world:

- **Google Cloud Platform**: Google Cloud Platform (GCP) is the cloud platform by Google. It uses the resources such as computers, hard disks, virtual machines, NoSQL databases, block storages, and so on located at Google data centers.

- **Amazon Web Services**: Then we have AWS. It is one of the safest, secure, and versatile cloud platforms that provides cloud services ranging from infrastructure services such as database storage, computing power, to networking. AWS provides you a wide variety of services not offered by any other cloud vendor - coming early in market has its own perks and downfalls.

- **Microsoft Azure**: Then we can Microsoft Azure, as name suggest it is by Microsoft. Microsoft Azure is also one of the front runners in grabbing market share. Azure has the potential to deploy and design applications with a huge network worldwide.

- **Adobe**: Adobe is often known for products such as Adobe Acrobat or Adobe Flash. But it also offers many products that provide cloud services. A few among them are Adobe Creative Cloud, Adobe Experience Cloud, and Adobe Document Cloud.

- **VMware**: VMware as we all know is a universal leader in virtualization. VMware also holds its space in cloud infrastructure to a better extent. Major features of VMware's cloud computing includes reduction in the IT intricacy, lowering expenses, and provides flexible, agile services.

- **IBM Cloud**: IBM is one of the other front runners in providing IaaS, PaaS, and SaaS. With IBM Cloud you can have the option to select and unite your desired tools, data models, and delivery models along with designing/creating your applications.

- **Rackspace**: Rackspace Cloud just like other cloud vendors offers many services such as hosting websites or web applications. They also provide services in uploading files in cloud, block storage, backup on cloud, databases, cloud servers, and many more.

- **Red Hat**: Open Cloud technology used by IT organizations is part of Red Hat cloud solutions. Agile and flexible solutions are delivered by RedHat. By modernizing the apps, updating and managing from a single place we can use Red Hat Cloud to integrate all the desired parts into a single solution.

- **Salesforce**: Salesforce Cloud Computing is another cloud vendor in the market. The major services that Salesforce provide are in the domain of CRM, ERP, customer service, and sales.
- **Oracle Cloud**: SaaS, PaaS, and IaaS - all deployment types are available with Oracle Cloud. The differentiation is Oracle Cloud is transforming customer's business quickly and reducing IT complexity. It is the speciality of Oracle Cloud.

Nippon Telegraph and Telephone, Atlantic.net, GoDaddy, 1 & 1, Digital Ocean, Cloud Sigma, and Navisite are a few other cloud service vendors in the market.

Now that we understood major aspects of cloud analytics let's understand the GCP infrastructure by watching below video.

Google Cloud Platform introduction—video

This video describes about Google Cloud Platform infrastructure across globe.

Link: `https://www.youtube.com/watch?v=pmq5rsL1AMc`

QR code:

After learning on a superficial level about the preceding different cloud vendors, different types of solutions they provide, and how they work, we are now going to focus on how to build an infrastructure on the cloud in a generic way, things that you need to be careful of, and how to build architecture.

Summary

In this chapter, we studied the basics of cloud computing, the different models we have, and what different service models we have.

We also studied security and the importance of security in cloud architecture.

Then I also introduced you to a few major cloud vendors, such as Google Cloud Platform, Amazon Web Services, and Microsoft Azure.

In the next chapter, we will study architecture at a better and elaborate level. This will give you a very precise idea about the cloud and how it works.

2
Design and Business Considerations

In this chapter, we will be learning about how cloud-based solutions are designed and architected. What should be our approach before the solution is moved to the cloud? We will also learn about whether we should consider on-premises hardware or directly move the solution to cloud. In short, we will be learning about the migration and related processes along with the prerequisite preparation required.

This chapter is going to discuss cloud computing in more depth too. Some concepts from previous chapters will be helpful to us as well.

We will cover the following topics in this chapter:

- Cloud computing and migration
- Parameters before adopting cloud strategy
- Prerequisites for an application to be moved to cloud
- Simplifying cloud migration with virtualization
- Infrastructure contemplation for cloud
- Available deployment models while moving to cloud
- Cloud migration checklist
- Architecture of cloud computing ecosystem
- Applications of cloud computing
- Preparing a plan for moving to cloud computing
- Making arrangements for a multi-provider methodology
- Technologies utilized by cloud computing

A bit more about cloud computing and migration

What began as cloud storage soon extended to incorporate services, for example, **Software as a Service (SaaS)**, which have developed into a stack of business-profitable *aaS* models including **Infrastructure as a Service (IaaS)**, **Platform as a Service (PaaS)**, **Database as a Service (DBaaS)**, **Data as a Service (DaaS)**, **Backup as a Service (BaaS)**, and **Disaster Recovery as a Service (DRaaS)**.

Close to the previous decade and a half, cloud services have quickly turned out to be a standout among the most noteworthy advancements in IT. The publicity encompassing cloud services made look as though all of an organization's IT assets ought to be immediately moved to the cloud. There is no disproving that, in specific cases, cloud services can be extremely advantageous. Be that as it may, cloud relocation maybe doesn't suit some cases.

Cloud may not be ideal for everything, but without a doubt it is important for everybody from numerous points of view. I foresee that most organizations will move far from on-premises later on. Not all workloads from the organizations may fit the cloud; however, most organizations can and should embrace cloud in some way or another. Empowering IT departments to optimize and streamline their IT delivery models and increase performance, these solutions are empowering IT to accomplish more with existing spending plans. Added to this, the organizations (and clients) demand on innovation in technology, the speed of implementation, and the pay-as-you-go-model, implies that an ever increasing number of organizations are implementing cloud services into their IT systems.

Cloud computing offers an incredible measure of business agility, cost improvements, and service efficiencies to managers. Be that as it may, for an organization to achieve a level where the cloud brings benefits is not a cakewalk. The inquiry thus moves towards becoming—*what do you have to do to remember when building up a cloud plan?*

Before you implement a cloud computing plan, you ought to gain understanding of the targets that are driving the embracing of cloud services, and framework necessities that must be met. The understanding of targets will give you a diagram and adjust the organization on the advantages that are normal.

Organizations need to investigate their very common investments in infrastructure (from the hardware to application portfolios, to network architecture and past) to decide whether the migration will be advantageous. A portion of the migration questions are technical, for example, regardless of whether a given application can perform sufficiently in the cloud; a few questions will include non-technical, financial issues example whether a cloud migration is cost-effective given current investments in infrastructure.

Here we find the aspects that should direct us with a cloud migration plan and help decide whether to move on-premises workloads to the cloud.

One of the primary contemplations would be an organization's prevailing data center investment. In spite of the availability of the technologies example server virtualization and so on, there are genuine costs associated with deploying on-premises servers. There are licensing costs involved, as well as expenses related to equipment utilization, support infrastructure, upkeep, depreciation, and upgradation for scaling. There is a dependably generous investment related with an on-premises server. Outsourcing a server's data and/or functionality to the cloud may mean relinquishing your on-premises investment unless an on-premises server can be intended.

In spite of this rip-and-replace way to deal with cloud migration, it may not go well in a financial sense for organizations that have a substantial investment in an on-premises data center—an organization can still advantage from migrating specific on-premises assets to the cloud.

Regardless of how durable the equipment is, any server equipment in the long run winds up out of date. Enterprise-class organizations by and large manage with this anticipated obsolescence by implementing an equipment maturation policy. An organization, for instance, may choose to resign servers after five years of usage. An organization could assimilate a cloud services roadmap into its equipment maturation policy. Doing as such permits IT teams to migrate on-premises IT assets to the cloud as opposed to moving them to more up to date equipment continuously.

The vision of utilizing the cloud services is by and large striking for smaller organizations and new businesses. In instance of a smaller organization, the utilization of cloud services gives access to enterprise-class equipment and fault-tolerant features that would some way or another be excessively costly and subsequently unaffordable for them. Likewise, new businesses can profit from cloud services since they can get their activities running rapidly without investing in on-premises data center assets.

With a multitude of choices offered, organizations have the elasticity to migrate certain facets of IT to the cloud as and when needed. Nonetheless, as with any venture, it is indispensable that the general plan/outline is concurred and parameters are characterized instead of applying solutions haphazardly.

Parameters before adopting cloud strategy

Organizations need to guarantee ideal quantifiable profit, the most elevated amount of security, and an incredible end user experience and the greater part of this must be really accomplished if time is invested first in a cloud computing plan. The following sections highlight some key contemplations that each organization should have in its plan.

Developing and changing business needs

Investments in on-premise, high specification technologies with noteworthy and profoundly scalable storage capacity and security abilities can be greatly unsafe nowadays as the vast majority of organizations are rapidly changing and developing the ways they provide their services. The plan and architecture that serves the present business necessities may achieve the edge capacity limit considerably faster than anticipated, or may not meet new business requirements approaching in a year or somewhere in vicinity, regardless of how much planning and anticipation has been completed. In the meantime, taking a look at cloud solutions for getting the same functionality and usefulness at a significantly lesser cost and the ability of cloud solutions to scale up or down the users and features at ease is vital to every growing organization.

Security of data

With an external provider (cloud provider) putting the business data on their data center, organizations are worried about where that data is actually being put away and what is going on with it. This is truly natural conduct as organizations today are intensely dependent on data for their operations to be able to smoothly function and subsequently, they need their data to be entirely isolated from the pariahs and kept in an extremely secured zone.

In addition to the security, 24/7 availability is likewise expected, which implies that there ought to be zero down time and the access to the data ought to be extremely fast as well. These perspectives are getting extremely critical with expanded success of cyber-attacks and the introduction of new enactments across the world. Having the correct level of security tools and processes in place ought to be a mandate for any cloud provider, yet you ought to dependably check your position additionally before signing an agreement with the cloud provider.

Right off the bat, understand the level of security measures in place. The essentials ought to at minimum include user verification, backup and restoration/data recovery methods set up, a firewall, regular security audits, and a breach notification policy. At that point, ensure you readiness while having the complete difference of what are your responsibilities and what are the cloud provider's responsibilities with regards to the data being put away. Also ensure that you have security policies set up particularly for cloud alternatives. You are obliged for your data and the new enactments will ensure you (as well as the cloud provider) have done the right due diligence before engaging the cloud provider.

Organizational requests on the in-house IT team

As the dependence on IT develops, the requests on the IT team likewise grow. In the mean time, the IT spending plans are not straightened out promptly to mirror this and henceforth, utilizing existing IT spending plans all the more significantly while sustaining its effective running is essential. The IT department can concentrate its projects on the all the more vital and pivotal business transformation projects by giving over a portion of the typical business as usual work. In any case, you should first work out what should be moved to the cloud, which deployment models will be utilized, and the timescales for doing this, with the goal that it is controllable for the in-house IT team.

Cloud deployment models—public cloud, private cloud, and hybrid cloud

A choice that the vast majority of organizations take a gander at to get the best from both private cloud and public cloud services is to put assets in a half and half arrangement, that is, a hybrid solution. This is achieved through a cloud administration platform that interfaces at least two clouds that might be the discrete entities. By being bound together, the organizations can profit by different deployment models. This is likewise a financially savvy choice as many public cloud services are less expensive than private cloud.

By utilizing a half and half model, the organizations are not entirely dependent on a private cloud, which will possibly spare a significant amount of cash. The business can utilize the private cloud to process data safely and the public cloud for hosting and facilitating openly accessible data and sharing a lot of assets. Along these lines, organizations can appreciate speedier data exchange while actualizing expanded protection for the prospectives required. This model likewise empowers the organizations to promptly incorporate with other cloud applications, giving the organizations significantly more noteworthy adaptability to move applications, assets, and data between the public and private clouds as the business advances.

Legally binding responsibilities

Indeed, even as utilizing a cloud service has such a huge number of advantages, any organization needs to keep up control of its data and access. Here are some crucial facts that you should remember while signing agreements with cloud providers:

- Even though you do not have to stress over what equipment your cloud provider runs its platform on, you ought to comprehend and know enough to ensure your cloud service is robust enough.
- You ought to comprehend what safety features are set up, how they oversee incidents, and how they react. Ensure incident reaction plans are set up to safeguard your business.
- You ought to likewise ensure that the **SLA** (**service level agreement**) offered by your cloud provider is appropriate for your organization. In the event that you are searching for **HA** (**high availability**), Always-On with the fewest blackouts and downtime, check the SLA offered.
- Likewise, ensure that the governing elements are met by the cloud supplier, for example, the present Data Protection Act, which will end up being the General Data Protection Regulation in May 2018. Or on the other hand, that they have an arrangement set up for the new enactment.
- It is likewise vital to ensure that you have your own procedures set up, for example, working with HR. Ensure that when an employee leaves the organization, all access to the organization systems and frameworks is expelled. This is a typical oversight made by associations with different cloud administrations being utilized at their end.

Prerequisites for an application to be moved to the cloud

In case of application servers, you ought to consider whether the application can work in the cloud with no glitches. Additionally, the application's execution must be thought about similarly.

Regularly, the compatibility is never a major issue for fresh applications that run on cutting-edge systems. Likewise, the execution shouldn't be an issue for such applications as the vast majority of cloud providers enable the hardware equipment assets to be assigned to hosted servers on an as-required mode. All things considered, there are two noteworthy contemplations that must be considered for such applications.

Performance

Despite the fact that you can arrange the hosted application server with hypothetically boundless compute and memory assets, the data transfer capacity of the web can at present hinder the application's general performance. It adds minimal value to have an elite hosted application server if web data transmission limitations impede a decent user experience.

Portability

Despite the fact that it is regularly simple to move a virtualized application server to the cloud, the application may have peripheral conditions that preclude (or essentially muddle) a cloud migration. For instance, the application may have an Active Directory reliance or expect access to an on-premises SQL server database.

For more established applications that run on legacy platforms, a move to the cloud may not be an alternative. Lab testing is the best way to know how an application will carry on in a cloud domain. Testing decides the means that are engaged with moving the application there.

Another thought for moving application servers to the cloud is equipment versatility. Some IT analysts propose that the cloud services are perfect for facilitating equipment serious workloads since cloud benefits by and large offer boundless versatility. While a cloud provider can, for the most part, scale its offerings to meet even the most severe workloads, this adaptability includes some considerable price.

Infrastructure as a Service (IaaS) suppliers, for example, Microsoft Azure and Amazon Web Services, charge clients an asset utilization based monthly expense, so a cloud-based elite computing environment can move towards becoming cost-restrictive.

Simplifying cloud migration with virtualization

Regardless of the extent of organization, one of the imperative contemplations is, whether the workloads focused for cloud movement have been virtualized. In a large portion of the cases, it's substantially less demanding to move workloads to the cloud if on-premises servers have just been virtualized. In all actuality, a portion of the cloud suppliers enables an organization to port their on-premise virtual machines straight on their platform. On the off chance that on-premises servers have not been virtualized, a movement to the cloud is likely still conceivable; however, the procedure may include more extreme work.

Infrastructure contemplation for cloud

Another contemplation is the on-premises network. On the off chance that an organization intends to keep assets on-premises (even briefly), the cloud network must function as an expansion of the on-premises Active Directory forests. This implies that the organization will ordinarily need to deploy cloud-based domain controllers, DNS servers, and perhaps DHCP servers. All the more imperatively, the organization ought to make sense of how to build up a safe data interchanges way between the cloud-based virtual network and the on-premises physical network.

This necessity, more often than not, is not a major issue for organizations with a current on-premises network; however, it implies that a lot of planning and preparation might be required before starting the movement procedure.

As an organization ponders the dangers and advantages of cloud relocation, it is essential to remember that cloud migrations are not a win bust recommendation. Organizations do not need to go *all in* with cloud transitions. Most of the time, it will bode well to move certain services to the cloud while proceeding to work with others on-premises.

Available deployment models while moving to cloud

We have three available deployment models while deploying to the cloud:

- The **Infrastructure as a Service** or the **IaaS** model
- The **Platform as a Service** or the **PaaS** model
- The **Software as a Service** or the **SaaS** model

We will be discussing the advantages and disadvantages of these deployment models in detail, in the following sections.

IaaS

IaaS enables the cloud provider to openly find an IT infrastructure over the web in a financially savvy way. Following image will help you to understand IaaS Architecture.

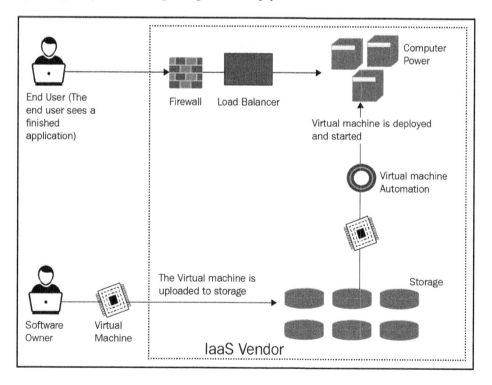

Advantages of IaaS

A portion of the key advantages of IaaS are as per the following:

- **Full control of the computing assets through authoritative access to VMs**: You can issue authoritative order to a cloud provider to run the virtual machine or to persist data on a cloud server. You can issue authoritative command to virtual machines that you possess to start the web server or to provision new applications. These are simply a couple of cases of managerial work you may do on the cloud assets; however, there are many more authoritative tasks that you can perform.
- **Adaptable and proficient leasing of PC equipment**: IaaS assets, for example, virtual machines, storage devices, data transmission, IP addresses, monitoring services, firewalls, and so on, are made accessible to you on rental mode. The payment depends on the measure of time the client holds or runs an asset relying upon its type. With authoritative access to virtual machines, you can run any software, even a custom OS, depending on your own software licenses.
- **Portability and interoperability with legacy applications**: It is conceivable to keep up legacy among applications and workloads between IaaS clouds. For instance, network applications, for example, web servers or email servers, which typically keep runs on your owned server equipment can likewise run within virtual machines in IaaS cloud.

Disadvantages of IaaS

IaaS has numerous advantages as we have examined, it also has its own particular issues that are as follows:

- **Compatibility with legacy safety susceptibilities**: As IaaS allows you to run legacy software in cloud provider's infrastructure, it opens you to the greater part of the security susceptibilities of such legacy software.
- **Virtual machine straggle**: Virtual Machines, now and again, can end up obsolete regarding security updates or patches as IaaS enables the client to work with the virtual machines in running, suspended, and off mode. The cloud provider can automatically update/patch such VMs, yet this procedure is intense and, to a great degree, very complex.

- **Toughness of Virtual Machine level isolation**: IaaS offers a disengaged environment to individual clients through hypervisor. Hypervisor is a software layer (middleware) that incorporates an equipment bolster for virtualization to part a physical computer into a number of virtual machines. You do not have any control on the conduct of the hypervisor as it is completely arranged and controlled by the cloud provider.
- **Data erase policies**: You utilize virtual machines that utilize the regular data storage assets given by the cloud provider. At whatever point you discharge the asset, the cloud provider must guarantee that the next consumer to lease the asset does not get the opportunity to watch any data deposit from past buyers (you, in this situation).

PaaS

PaaS is a blend of IaaS and an arrangement of middleware, software development, and development tools that enable the organization to make, create, and deploy on cloud up to speed and scale.

Following image will help you understand PaaS:

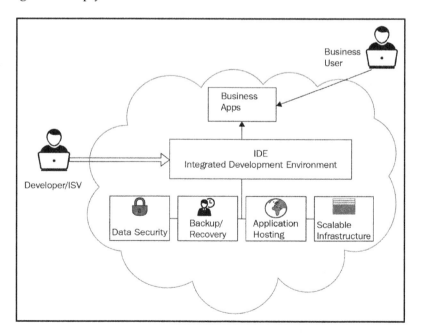

Advantages of PaaS

A few of the key advantages of PaaS are as follows:

- **Minor authoritative burden**: You do not have to fret over the IT and software platform administration as it is the commitment of the cloud provider.
- **Less price of possession**: You don't have to buy costly equipment, servers, power, data storage devices, and so on.
- **Versatile and flexible solutions**: Scaling assets up or down, in or out, or automatically in view of user load whenever needed is utterly simple.
- **Up to date and patched system software**: Cloud provider is exclusively accountable for patching and upgrading the system software for you without breaking your deployments by any means. This is extremely imperative as it shields your deployments from regularly developing safety dangers.

Disadvantages of PaaS

Like **IaaS**, **PaaS** also has its own particular issues that are as follows:

- **Portability and compatibility across different cloud providers**: In spite of the fact that the programming languages, software development frameworks, and so on that are utilized to build up the applications might be common, yet the platform implementations may contrast starting with one cloud provider then onto the next. This influences migration/movement of the workloads starting with one cloud provider then onto the next, which is amazingly mind boggling. To put it plainly, PaaS-based arrangements are firmly coupled to the cloud provider.
- **Event-based scheduling of computing assets**: The PaaS-based applications are event-oriented and this postures asset requirements on these applications as they ought to answer a demand in a pre-characterized interval of time.
- **Architecting safety of applications and data deployed on PaaS**: PaaS-based applications should unequivocally actualize cryptography and oversee safety exposures as they are altogether relied on the network.

SaaS

SaaS is a business application developed and hosted by a service provider. In this model, clients don't have any activity on the environment and the service provider deals with the whole foundation and furthermore the application. The clients are charged in view of the use of the application and its services (pay as you go billing model).

For fruitful cloud selection, you first need to profoundly comprehend your IT environment by recognizing those workloads that will best fit your targeted cloud environment, while additionally giving you a steady profit for your speculation.

The following image will help you understand SaaS:

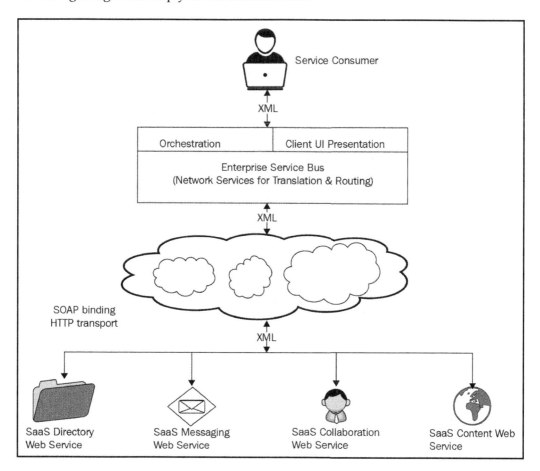

Cloud migration checklist

You have to make sure that the following aspects are in place while going ahead with cloud migration:

- **Influence on business**: You shouldn't begin the migration procedure with mission critical applications for the business. In the event that the business is a retail business, you shouldn't move internet business straight away. Or maybe, you should gain more understanding of cloud by first moving less critical supporting applications (for example, departmental applications, email servers, intranets, and so forth) to cloud.
- **Deployment environments**: Clearly you will initially think about your less critical environments (for example, development environments and test environments), yet ensure you think about the production environment when you configure your test environment particularly. We prescribe you to utilize the very same configuration for test environments that your production environment will use.
- **Significance of performance**: You shouldn't consider environments that require intense data handling or the exceedingly performance intensive applications. Your customers may dump your application(s) and move to a contender, in the event that they confront relentless execution issues.
- **Complex systems**: The systems with impressively complex design that have different endpoints of integration between and across applications should be kept away from an underlying level of migration. The explanation behind this is the configuration on the cloud is practically not the same as on-premises deployments and the movement of complex systems may require part of changes and alterations on cloud, which needs some genuine research and study.
- **Contemplation of licensing**: Examination of your cloud seller's licensing model is critical to check whether it would be expensive contrasted with your on-premises licensing.
- **Contemplation of service level agreement**: It is critical for you to examine that the SLA wanted by your system is upheld by your cloud seller.

- **Contemplation of safety**: Another critical thought is to investigate if your cloud seller underpins all the safety compliances required by your business.
- **Contemplation of platform**: You likewise need to examine the equipment (hardware platform) support given by your cloud seller as your system may have reliance on some particular sort of equipment (for example, CPU vendor, 32-bit/64-bit, and so on.). Also, examine the **operating systems (OSes)** accessible with your cloud seller as your system may have a reliance on OS as well.
- **Location of data (where it is hosted)**: Location of data hosting is another critical thought, as a few nations don't permit to have your data outside your nation and subsequently, you need to ensure that your cloud seller has a data center inside the nation of your business.
- **System preparedness**: Is your system prepared for cloud deployment or do you have to redesign and remake it?

Architecture of a cloud computing ecosystem

In a cloud computing ecosystem, there are a number of computers, servers, and data storage equipment that together make the *cloud* of computing services. Cloud computing could incorporate any program (from data handling applications, to enterprise scale applications, to computer games). For the most part, every application has its own committed server paying little mind to the cloud provider you utilize.

To guarantee that everything works smoothly and proficiently, the cloud ecosystem utilizes a focal server (otherwise known as control server) to administer and monitor traffic and customer requests, which eventually includes the utilization of protocols (set of rules) and middleware (special software). The reason why middleware is utilized here is to permit different networked computers in the ecosystem to exchange information with each other.

The following image can help you understand all the aspects that cloud computing has:

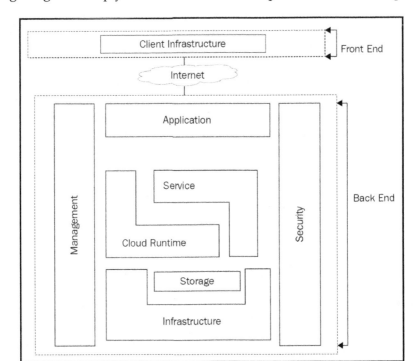

As a general rule, you will find that a large portion of the servers and computers and so forth, don't work at full limit, which implies that there are parts of assets (such as compute power, data storage limit, and so on) going to waste as they are staying unused. Cloud computing utilizes different server virtualization technologies to make these valuable unused assets by transforming them into a number of virtual servers with every one of them running with their own autonomous operating systems. The server virtualization, truth be told, lessens the prerequisite of more physical servers as it augments the yield of individual physical servers.

Presently, here comes a genuine test. The servers and different devices have the likelihood of breakdowns like some other computers. On the off chance that such a breakdown happens (it is uncommon, yet at the same time conceivable) the valuable information of cloud buyers might be lost. Now and again, it might be only the inaccessibility of the cloud applications and services.

In any of these cases, there will be colossal misfortunes acquired by the organizations running their applications, services, data storage, and so forth on the cloud. Consequently, it is vital for the cloud providers to have the whole cloud system set up in a repetitive way. This implies running the entire ecosystem in parallel on another arrangement of networked servers and different devices. If there should be an occurrence of breakdown, the control server can get to the reinforcement (parallel) ecosystem to make the applications, services, data storage, and so on open to its clients. This is the place that the cloud computing brings in a dependable and robust IT framework.

To empower this reinforcement ecosystem, the cloud provider may need no less than double the quantity of equipment, which empowers no less than one reinforcement ecosystem. Kindly note that the more equipment your cloud provider presents, the more reinforcement ecosystems can be provisioned, which eventually takes the unwavering quality and reliability factor to more elevated amounts.

Infrastructure for cloud computing

The cloud computing infrastructure includes servers, storage devices, networks, administration software, deployment software, and virtualization platforms.

Have a look at the parameters in the following image:

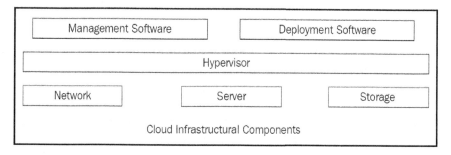

The functions of these parameters are as follows:

- **Administration Software**: Keeps up and arranges the infrastructure.
- **Deployment Software**: Helps to deploy and incorporate applications on the cloud.
- **Hypervisor**: A firmware that goes about as a Virtual Machine Manager, which permits sharing of a single physical instance of cloud assets over various tenants.

- **Network**: The key segment of cloud infrastructure that permits connecting cloud services over the web. It is, for the most part, adaptable by the client in terms of network protocols and routes and so forth.
- **Server**: Processes asset sharing requirements and offers different services, for example, asset allotment and de-allotment, monitoring the assets, ensuring safety, and so on.
- **Storage**: As the name suggests, it is in charge of storing the data. For higher unwavering quality, cloud keeps up various copies of it, so that in the event that one of the storage assets dies, the data can still be made accessible from another.

Constrictions on cloud infrastructure

The following parameters have to be considered while implementing the cloud infrastructure:

- **Transparency**: Virtualization is the way to share assets in a cloud environment. Be that as it may, it isn't conceivable to fulfil the request with single assets or servers. Along these lines, there must be straightforwardness in assets, load balancing, and applications, so we can scale them on request.
- **Scalability**: Scaling up an application deployment is not that simple as scaling up an application, since it includes setup overhead or even re-architecting the network. In this manner, an application deployment is required to be adaptable with the end goal that the assets can be provisioned and de-provisioned effortlessly in view of interest and henceforth we require the virtual infrastructure.
- **Smart monitoring**: To accomplish straightforwardness and versatility in a solid way, an application deployment should be equipped for smart monitoring.
- **Safety**: The super server (data center) in the cloud ought to be safely architected. Additionally, the control node, an entry point in super server, likewise should be exceedingly safe.

Applications of cloud computing

Accordingly, there is no restriction for uses of cloud computing. With the exact middleware set up, the cloud computing ecosystem can run each kind of program that a regular computer system can run. The kind of projects that cloud computing ecosystem underpins, run from straightforward spreadsheet software to highly tweaked enterprise scale software.

At this moment, an imperative inquiry is the reason you, me, or any other individual might want to depend on an outsider's computing ecosystem to run software and store information. We should observe a few reasons for this, as follows:

- Your clients can get to their information and applications from any place and whenever they need to. The clients would simply require any web empowered device (desktop PC, laptop, tablet PC, smart phone, kiosk, and so on). The applications and information would not be limited to a particular hard drive on a particular client's device or an internal network server of any corporate network.
- Cloud computing does not require any progressed and high configuration equipment on customer side as it itself can deal with these requirements for the customer. You can have a fundamental device having sufficient compute power only to run the middleware necessary to communicate with the cloud ecosystem. This implies that the general cost of usage would be significantly low.
- Organizations that depend on computers for their operations need to ensure that they have the right software set up to accomplish their objectives. The cloud computing ecosystems enable these organizations to give expansive access to different software they utilize. The organizations may pick the "Pay as you go" payment model (utilization-based payment model) rather than purchasing various software or software licenses. This additionally enables the general cost to be cut down extensively.
- In the event that you want to set up your own data centers (this is alluded as on-premises setup), you would require physical space to have this setup done. It is possible that you would purchase this space or you would take it on rent. Regardless, this implies significant speculation is required. With cloud computing, you have a choice of putting away your information and deploying your applications on a cloud provider's equipment, killing the requirement for physical space totally (for the data center).
- This additionally implies that you can spare more cost as you don't require a separate team for the equipment upkeep as the required equipment would be kept up by your cloud provider.
- The organizations can exploit the whole computing power of the network if the cloud ecosystem is based on the highest point of grid computing by the cloud provider. This can be truly helpful for profoundly serious applications.

Preparing a plan for moving to cloud computing

As we discussed previously, before you prepare a plan for moving to cloud, it is critical to think about your real business prerequisites. We will now have a quick recap of a few of the essential prerequisites:

- Available/approved finances
- Cloud deployment model—public, private, hybrid
- Data safety and confidentiality
- Data reinforcement
- Dashboards and reports
- Client accessibility
- Data distribution and integration
- Readiness of staff for adopting cloud computing

It is critical to do plenty of preparation and planning while wanting to meet these prerequisites, which, for the most part, run with three essential stages.

Methodology stage

It is critical for you to examine the methodology issues that you may confront. This examination is done based on:

- Cloud computing proposal worth
- Cloud computing methodology planning

The following image can explain strategies diagrammatically:

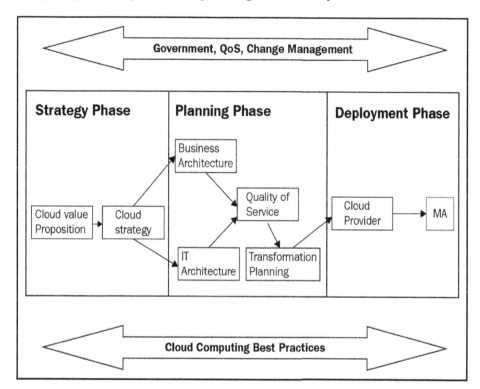

Cloud computing proposal worth

Here, you have to do the profound examination of the aspects that impact you while applying mode of cloud computing and after that target the key issues you wish to determine. A portion of the key elements are:

- Making IT administration simpler
- Lessening of total price for operations and up keep of equipment and software
- Development in mode of business
- Cheaper contract out hosting with top class QoS (Quality of Service)

This investigation would help you with making decisions for future advancement.

Cloud computing methodology planning

You ought to build up the cloud computing methodology in view of past investigation outcomes. While applying cloud computing mode you may confront a few conditions in view of which you should set up a methodology document.

Planning stage

In this stage, you should play out a point by point investigation of issues and dangers in the cloud application to guarantee that the cloud computing is effectively meeting your business objectives. The prevalent planning steps are included here:

1. **Building business design**: Perceive the dangers that may be caused by a cloud computing application from a business point of view.
2. **Working on IT design**: Recognize the applications that help business processes and the technologies required to help enterprise applications and information systems.
3. **Creating necessities on Quality of Service (QoS)**: Quality of service alludes to the non-operational necessities, for example, dependability, safety, disaster management, and so on. The accomplishment of applying cloud computing mode relies upon these non-operational elements.
4. **Creating plan for conversion (Migration to cloud computing)**: Figure out a wide range of plans that are required to convert ongoing business to modes of cloud computing.

Distribution stage

In this stage, you should center around both of the past stages (methodology stage and planning stage). Furthermore, you have to consider:

- **Choice of cloud provider**: You should choose a cloud provider in light of service level agreement offered by it. The level of service offered by the provider is characterized by its SLA.
- **Upkeep and technical assistance**: The cloud provider needs to guarantee the QoS as upkeep and technical assistance are its responsibilities.

The following image is the cloud adoption framework that is suggested by Gartner:

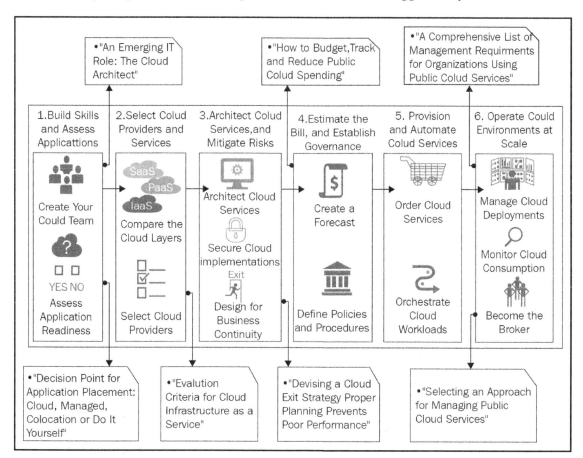

Making arrangements for a multi-provider methodology

A multi-provider methodology offers the chance to coordinate every application with the most fitting provider. It additionally offers hazard disaggregation by decreasing provider hook up. Organizations that are hoping to choose the perfect cloud provider, regularly request that to think about and pick the provider that is most appropriate for their applications. AWS, Microsoft Azure, and Google Cloud Platform are the major cloud providers in the IaaS offerings, and the greater part of requests made to Gartner about IaaS providers identify with them.

In that capacity, Gartner has assessed these providers through in-depth assessments in view of their *Evaluation Criteria for Cloud Infrastructure as a Service*. These reports are distributed yearly by Gartner and it is recommended to examine them before choosing the cloud provider.

Making a multi-provider design tactic

While making a multi-supplier deign tactic, you should first settle on how they plan to utilize different cloud suppliers. Potential methodologies incorporate the accompanying:

- Use diverse workloads with different cloud providers
- Use a similar workload over different cloud providers
- Use one cloud provider for production use, and another cloud provider for disaster management

Technologies utilized by cloud computing

Cloud computing relies upon a few base technologies that make it exceptionally adaptable, dependable, solid, reusable, and financially savvy. These base technologies are:

- Grid computing
- Service-oriented architecture
- Virtualization
- Utility computing

We will discuss each of them in the following sections.

Grid computing

This refers to a highly distributed computing model in which a group of computers and computing devices from various locations are interconnected to each other and each of them configured to contribute their unutilized resources to form a much bigger computing system to do some heavy processing. The location of the contributing computing devices or computers could be geographically discrete and even the type of devices/computers could be heterogeneous as well. These resources, thus, form a huge computing grid just like the electricity grids.

Basically, grid computing breaks down much complex tasks into smaller and simpler tasks based on some predefined configuration policy and then these smaller tasks are distributed to CPUs that are present in the grid, and thus, improving the overall performance.

The following image can help you understand more about Grid Computing.

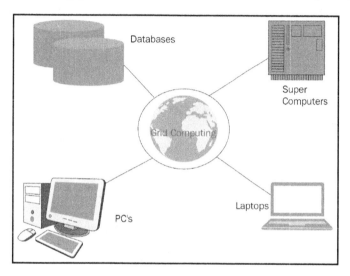

Service-oriented architecture

The principle behind **service-oriented architecture** (**SOA**) is to allow using applications as a service by other applications regardless of the platform (type of vendor, product, or technology) being used on either side (service and service consumer). This allows communication and data exchange between applications built on heterogeneous platforms without the need of any additional programming or making changes to the services. What we look for here is seamless integration between any type of applications.

Following image can help you understand more about SOA:

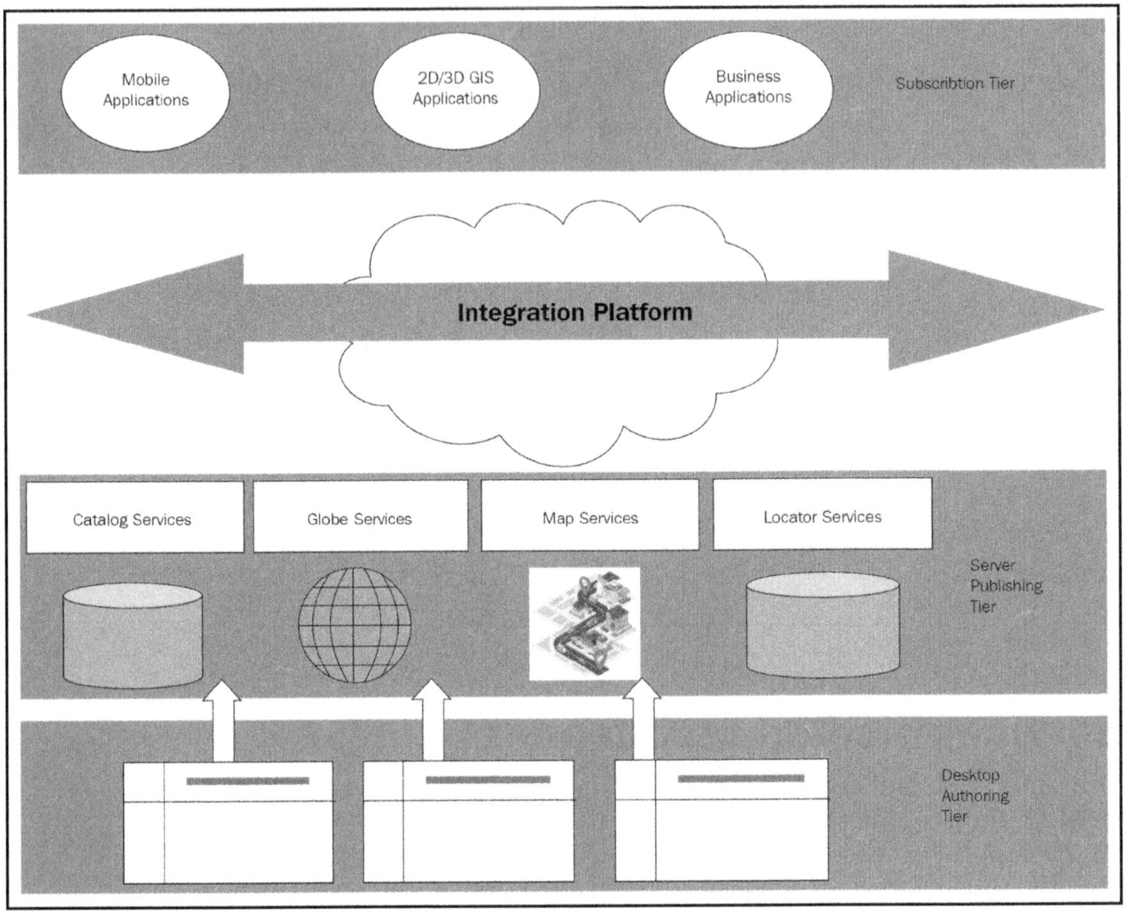

Virtualization

It is a technology that allows us to share a single physical instance of an application or computing resource among multiple organizations or individual customers, collectively known as tenants, and the architecture itself is known as multitenant architecture. To do this it assigns a logical name to a physical resource and providing a pointer to that physical resource when demanded. The multitenant architecture offers virtual isolation among the multiple tenants. Hence, the organizations can use and customize their application as though they each have their individual and isolated instances running.

The following image can help you understand more about Virtualization:

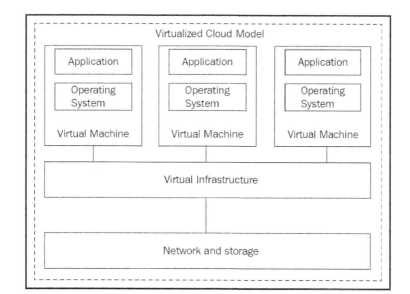

Utility computing

It is based on a pay-per-use model (pay as you go model). It offers computational resources on demand as a metered service. Cloud computing, grid computing, and managed IT services are based on this concept. This plays an extremely important role in setting up the billing of cloud applications.

Summary

In this chapter, we have learned about the parameters and prerequisites for adopting a cloud computing platform for your organization. We have also learned about the available cloud deployment models and their features, advantages, and disadvantages.

In the next chapter, we will be discussing one of the most prominent cloud services in detail—the Google Cloud Platform.

3

GCP 10,000 Feet Above – A High-Level Understanding of GCP

In this chapter, we are going to dive into the Google Cloud Platform and all its components. This chapter will give a better purpose of GCP tools. We are going to categorize all the GCP tools and then understand each of them in brief. Along with gaining complete understanding of the services, we will also gain knowledge of differences between the tools, such as two tools that might be serving the same purpose. Then I will be explaining the major differences and use cases that you will using that tool in.

The following this chapter, we will have a deep dive into all the major services that GCP provides. For now, this will be the first chapter completely focused on Google Cloud Platform.

As we understand the utility of these components, we will gain insight into a complete GCP ecosystem.

We will cover the following topics in this chapter:

- Different services offered by typical cloud vendors
- Understanding cloud categories

Different services offered by typical cloud vendors

Before starting with GCP, let's try to understand the service categorization by major competitors of GCP, that is, **Amazon Web Services (AWS)** and Microsoft Azure.

First let's get started with AWS. AWS has 21 broad categories, namely Compute, Storage, Database, Migration, Network and Content Delivery, Developer Tools, Management Tools, Media Services, Machine Learning, Analytics, Security Identity and Compliance, Mobile Service, AR and VR, Application Integration, Customer Engagement, Business Productivity, Desktop and App Streaming, Internet of Things, Game Development, and Software and Cost Management.

Similarly, Azure has categorized services into 13 parts, namely Compute, Networking, Storage, Web and Mobile, Containers, Databases, Analytics, AI and Machine Learning, Internet of Things, Enterprise Integration, Security and Identity, Developer Tools, and Management Tools.

If you have a close look at the naming mechanism of both the vendors, you will find at least eight categories having the same or very similar names.

Now, we are going to see what GCP has to offer us with this. GCP has close to 11 different categories, and they are the following:

- Compute
- Storage and Databases
- Networking
- Big Data
- Data Transfer
- Cloud AI
- API Platforms and Ecosystems
- Identity and Security
- Management Tools
- Developer Tools
- Internet of Things

The picture is very clear now—almost all cloud vendors have the same or very similar terminologies to all the services they provide. The reason for this? To make it more appealing and more accessible to the consumer. If we as consumers are jumping from one vendor to another, the naming should not be a constraint in terms of generic categories at least.

But if we try to explore the specific names of the services then there is a huge gap with naming conventions between all the vendors. And that is legally required.

So now that we know broadly the different categories of GCP, we will start exploring each of them and all the services they comprise.

Understanding cloud categories

Now, as we have seen the 11 broad categories of the services in GCP, we will try to understand each of them. The following table specifies the different features of these categories:

Cloud category	Features
Compute	• High-performance, scalable VMs • Build apps, scale automatically • Automated container management • Private docker container images • Serverless applications on Google's infrastructure
Storage and databases	• Managed databases • Object storage • Archival
Networking	• Worldwide autoscaling and load balancing • Manage networking for your resources • Highly available global DNS network • Fast, high availability interconnect • Content delivery network
Big data	• Analytics data warehouse • Batch and stream data processing • Managed Hadoop and Spark • Powerful data exploration • Tell great data stories to support better business decisions • Intelligent data preparation • Scalable event ingestion and messaging middleware
Data transfer	• Online transfer • Cloud storage transfer service • Transfer appliance beta • BigQuery data transfer service

Cloud AI	• Train custom machine learning models • Hardware optimized for machine learning • Large scale machine learning service • Powerful job search and discovery • Create conversational experiences across devices and platforms • Powerful video analysis • Powerful image analysis • Powerful speech recognition • Powerful text analysis • Fast, dynamic translation
API platforms and ecosystems	• Provides access to numerous APIs • Performs API analytics • Supports API monetization
Identity and security	• Manages encryption keys • User access control • Full control over security
Management tools	• Integrated monitoring, logging, and diagnostics • Full-Stack monitoring, powered by Google • Real-time log management and analysis • Real-time exception monitoring and alerting • Detailed performance insights • Detailed performance insights and analytics • Simplify your cloud management • Manage your APIs • Powerful web admin UI • Your Google curated admin machine • Cloud platform in a mobile app • Google cloud billing API documentation • Google cloud APIs
Developer tools	• Essential tools for cloud platform • Simplify your cloud management • Collaborative development on GIT • Make IntelliJ your cloud platform IDE • PowerShell on Google cloud platform • Visual Studio as your cloud platform IDE • Firebase test lab for Android
Internet of Things	• Help you connect sensors to cloud

Now that we have understood the complete motto of each and every category, we will now be focusing on the components that each category holds.

Compute

The following are the services that fall under the Compute category:

- Compute engine
- App engine
- Kubernetes engine
- Cloud function

We will discuss each of them in the coming sections.

Compute Engine

The main purpose of Compute Engine is to provide readily available virtual machines—that are highly scalable, high with performance. Using Compute Engine you can set up your own server—on Linux or Windows.

You can create your custom VM and load your application atop it.

When to use:

If you want the complete machine to be customized with your own software, applications, and configurations of your own you can opt for Compute Engine VMs.

Special features:

- The VMs come with per second billing
- You can build your custom VM with max 96 vCPU and 624 GB of RAM

Costing:

To learn more about costing you can refer to the following link.

Costing for Cloud Compute: https://cloud.google.com/compute/pricing.

App engine

Whenever we want to build a web app or an Android app, we always have to think of the frontend, APIs, and backend infrastructure. But now using App Engine all we have to worry about is the code we are writing for our app. Leave the headache of infrastructure to GCP.

When to use:

If your team lack in infrastructure competencies, you have requirement of load balancing, or want enabling of auto scaling; these are a few of the scenarios when you can opt for App Engine.

Special features:

- Supports almost all popular languages
- No need to think of infrastructure
- Auto scalable
- Load Balancer enabled
- High Security

Costing:

To learn more about costing you can refer to the following link.

Costing for App Engine: https://cloud.google.com/appengine/pricing.

Kubernetes engine

If you want to deploy your containerized application and also want to manage it then Kubernetes Engine is the perfect solution for you. Kubernetes Engine can help us to scale a containerized application to be deployed, updated, and managed anywhere in any environment. Kubernetes Engine is used to deploy Docker as well.

When to use:

You can use Docker if you want to have a version control system for an entire application OS. Kubernetes can also be used when you have your application in Docker going through many phases, such as test, build, and dev and managing it becomes tough.

Special features:

The following are the special features of Kubernetes Engine:

- You can Auto Upgrade, Auto Repair, and Auto Scale
- Supports Docker Image
- Fully managed
- Supports IAM

Costing:

Kubernetes Engine charges are done according to the Compute Engine VM price as per each machine in the cluster. Thus, its costing is done according to the Compute Engine pricing at `https://cloud.google.com/compute/pricing`.

Cloud function

This service is in Beta stage at the time of writing. Cloud Function assists us in building Serverless Applications. With serverless applications, as the name suggests, we do not own any server (or any infrastructure as such) of our own. The infrastructure will come into the picture only when customers have a demand of it. If the application has not been accessed by any person in the last 10 hours then you won't be charged for that. Plus it is fully managed!

When to use:

If you want to have a backend to your mobile or want to collect IoT data over GCP Pub/Sub and send it to a database, these are the perfect scenarios for using Cloud Function.

Special features:

The following are the special features of Cloud Function:

- API and Microservices provided
- Connection to Cloud Storage available
- Respond to HTTP/S requests
- Logging, Monitoring, and Debugging enabled

Costing:

Cloud Function has a Free Tier and a Paid Tier. You get some storage, requests, and compute time free every month. If you exceed it, you will get billed. The following table might help you understand this:

	Free limit per month	Price above free limit (per unit)	Price unit
Invocations	2 million invocations	$0.40	per million invocations
Compute Time	400,000 GB-seconds	$0.0000025	per GB-Second
	200,000 GHz seconds	$0.0000100	per GHz-Second
Outbound Data (Egress)	5GB	$0.12	per GB
Inbound Data (Ingress)	Unlimited	Free	per GB
Outbound Data to Google APIs in same region	Unlimited	Free	per GBUse case

Storage and databases

The services falling under the Storage and Databases category are as follows:

- Cloud Storage
- Cloud SQL
- Cloud Bigtable
- Cloud Spanner
- Cloud Datastore
- Persistent Disk

Let's discuss each of them in the following sections.

Cloud storage

Databases support certain kinds of file formats, can manage data of a certain size, and are costly to make multi-regional. So when you need these features in your infrastructure you can opt for Cloud Storage. On Cloud Storage, you can store any kind of data, such as movies, songs, text files, and live and archival data. This data is called object—just object; no file format or no size.

When to use:

Data availability is a must have, archiving PBs of data on a stringent budget, and good security—reasons to use Cloud Storage. You can also host your website on Cloud Storage and chances are it will be free!

Special features:

- Archives cold data
- Builds websites and mobile apps
- Very low storing cost
- Analyzes existing data

Costing:

Please refer to the following table for details about the costing of Cloud Storage:

	Access frequency	At rest pricing	Retrieval pricing	Monthly uptime*
Multi-Regional	Frequent, Cross-regional	$0.026 per GB/month	Free	>= 99.95%
Regional	Frequent, Single-region	$0.02 per GB/month	Free	>= 99.9%
Nearline	Less than once per month	$0.01 per GB/month	$0.01 per GB	>= 99.0%
Coldline	Less than once per year	$0.007 per GB/month	$0.05 per GB	>= 99.0%

Cloud SQL

Cloud SQL provides fully managed MySQL and PostgreSQL. PostgreSQL is in Beta right now. You can use Cloud SQL as your backend database for your application. They can scale, and are secure and highly available.

When to use:

A major utility of Cloud SQL will be when you want a fully managed SQL database, leaving you to concentrate completely on the application. Cloud SQL is highly secure as well as SSAE 16, ISO 27001, PCI DSS v3.0, and HIPAA compliant. Discounts are an add on benefit when using it for a long duration.

Special features:

- Fully managed
- High Performance and Scalable
- Provides 99.95% availability

Costing:

Please refer to the following table for details about the costing of Cloud SQL:

Item	Standard pricing	With 100% sustained use discount
Cloud SQL Instance from 600MB to 416GB RAM	$0.0150—$8.0480 per hour	$0.0105- $5.6336 per hour
Storage	• $0.17 per GB/mo PD SSD • $0.09 per GB/mo PD Standard • $0.08 per GB/mo for backups	Sustained Use Discounts do not apply
Network	Ingress, Free	Sustained Use Discounts do not apply

To learn more about costing, you can refer to the following link.

Other supported region costing, `https://cloud.google.com/sql/pricing`.

Cloud Bigtable

Cloud Bigtable is one of the best NoSQL available on the market. Google uses Cloud Bigtable for Search, Maps, and Gmail. The scale at which we can have a seamless interaction with this NoSQL is a mesmerizing experience.

When to use:

If you want a fully managed NoSQL, which is well integrated with other GCP data processing and storage components.

Special features:

- Redundant Autoscaling Storage without paying extra
- Compatible and integrated with HBase, Spark, and Hadoop
- Global Availability
- Low latency with an unbelievable number

Costing:

Please refer to the following table for details about the costing of Cloud Bigtable:

Feature	Price
Nodes	$0.65 node/hour
SSD Storage	$0.17 (GB/month)
HDD Storage	$0.026 (GB/month)
Network Ingress	Free
Network Egress	Cross-region and internet egress rates apply

To learn more about costing and for other supported regions costing, you can refer to the following link: `https://cloud.google.com/bigtable/pricing`.

Cloud Spanner

Cloud Spanner is a database that is enterprise-grade, globally-distributed, and strongly consistent providing the taste of structure of relational database and horizontal scale of NoSQL, DBs—and it's one of its kind in the market.

It provides the best features of a relational database and non-relational database.

When to use:

If the application is having the requirement of having a schema, running SQL, having consistency, high availability and scalability along with replication—probably Cloud Spanner is the best solution.

Special features:

	Cloud spanner	Traditional relational	Traditional non-relational
Schema	Yes	Yes	No
SQL	Yes	Yes	No
Consistency	Strong	Strong	Eventual
Availability	High	Failover	High

Scalability	Horizontal	Vertical	Horizontal
Replication	Automatic	Configurable	Configurable

Costing:

Please refer to the following table for details about the costing of Cloud Spanner:

Feature	Regional price (USD)	Multi-region price (USD)
Nodes	From $0.90 per node per hr	From $3.00 per node per hr
Storage	From $0.30 per GB per month	From $0.50 per GB per month
Network Ingress	Free	
Network Egress	Cross-region and internet egress rates apply	

Cloud Datastore

Cloud Datastore is a highly scalable NoSQL database providing features such as automatic sharding and replication and it is highly durable and available. Cloud Datastore being a NoSQL provides us with ACID properties, SQL queries for simplicity, and indexes to get faster results.

When to use:

If you want a fully-managed NoSQL that supports SQL queries and is integrated to other GCP components.

Special features:

- Easy Query language
- Rich Admin Dashboard
- Supports ACID transaction
- Supports all possible datatypes

Costing:

Please refer to the following table for details about the costing of Cloud Datastore for the Iowa region:

	Free limit per day	Price above free limit (per unit)	Price unit
Stored data	1 GB storage	$0.18	GB/Month
Entity Reads	50,000	$0.06	per 100,000 entities
Entity Writes	20,000	$0.18	per 100,000 entities
Entity Deletes	20,000	$0.02	per 100,000 entities
Small Operations	50,000	Free	-

To learn more about costing you can refer to the following link.

Costing for Cloud Spanner -https://cloud.google.com/spanner/pricing.

Persistent Disk

Persistent Disk is the component that is lying below most of the services for storage. One major service extensively using Persistent Disk is Virtual Machines in Google Compute Engine. Persistent Disk are distinguished in different types such as Hard Disk Drive and Solid State Disk.

When to use:

Everytime you require a storage with your application using virtual machines.

Special features:

- Single disk can be as huge as 64 TB
- Attach and detach volumes as per requirements
- Create snapshots easily
- Encryption enabled

Costing:

To learn more about costing you can refer to the following link.

Costing for Persistent Disk: `https://cloud.google.com/datastore/pricing`

Type	Price (per GB / month)
Standard provisioned space	$0.040
SSD provisioned space	$0.170
Local SSD provisioned space (min 375GB disk)	$0.080
Snapshot storage	$0.026
IO operations	No additional charge

Networking

Now we are going to discuss the services falling under the Networking category, which are:

- Virtual Private Cloud (VPC)
- Cloud Load Balancing
- Cloud CDN
- Cloud Interconnect
- Cloud DNS
- Network Service Tiers ALPHA

We will discuss each of them in the following sections.

Virtual Private Cloud

Virtual Private Cloud has a main purpose of building your own private network as it is on the GCP—along with IP addresses, subnets, availability zone, and load balancers.

When to use:

While migrating your data this is going to be very useful, as you need to replicate the in-house network to the cloud.

Special features:

The following are the special features of VPC:

- VPN: Securely and easily connect your VPC network using IPsec
- Security: Provides great level of Firewall security
- Easy routing: Can route requests from one instance to another in the same network as well in subnet without external IPs

Costing:

To learn more about costing you can refer to the following link.

Ingress and Egress Pricing: `https://cloud.google.com/compute/pricing#network`

Please refer to the following table for details about the costing of VPN for the Iowa region:

Component billed	Price (USD)
Per tunnel (per hour)	$0.050
IPsec traffic	Charged the same as if it wasn't in a VPN tunnel. See `General network pricing`.
Public IP for VPN Gateway	Charged according to `IP address pricing`.

To learn more about costing you can refer to the following link.

Costing to VPN: `https://cloud.google.com/compute/pricing#network`.

Please refer to the following table for details about the costing of an IP address for the Iowa region:

Type	Price/hour
Static IP address (assigned but unused)	$0.010
Static IP address (assigned and in use)	No charge
Ephemeral IP address (attached to instance or forwarding rule)	No charge

To learn more about costing you can refer to the following link.

Costing of IP Address: `https://cloud.google.com/compute/pricing#network`.

Cloud load balancing

The Cloud Load Balancing service is used to provide auto scaling and load balancing to your application at great performance and scale.

When to use:

If you have customers using your application from geographically different locations and there are chances of unprecedented demand in resources anytime then you should opt to enable Cloud Load Balancing.

Special features:

- **Seamless Autoscaling**: In case of huge demand of resources your application will expand flawlessly and without any intervention required
- **HTTP(S) Load Balancing**: This helps us in balancing traffic across regions or availability zones on HTTP(S), while your application is accessible through a single IP
- **TCP/SSL and UDP support**: Cloud Load Balancing also supports TCP/SSL and UDP traffic

Costing:

To learn more about costing you can refer to the following link.

Costing for Cloud Load Balancing: `https://cloud.google.com/compute/pricing#lb`

Cloud CDN

Cloud CDN stands for **Cloud Content Delivery Network**. This is used when you have a huge global audience to serve your content.

When to use:

A video library that has some of the most vintage videos from India and they are proprietary to that website, but the audience is based out of Japan, Australia, or Israel. In that case, we can use Cloud CDN to serve our video content to a wide audience.

Special features:

- **Anycast**: Single IP for application
- **Invalidation**: Takes down cached content in minutes
- **HTTP/2 and HTTPS**: Supports HTTP/2 and provide us our SSL/TLS certificate

Costing:

Please refer to the following table for details about the costing of Cloud CDN:

Item	Price (USD)
Cache egress	Charges vary based on location and usage: $0.02/GB—$0.08/GB for North America and Europe destinations $0.04/GB—$0.20/GB for other destinations worldwide
Cache fill	Charges vary based on location: $0.04/GB—$0.06/GB discounted pricing for in-region cache fills $0.08/GB—$0.15/GB for cross-region cache fills
HTTP(S) requests	$0.0075 per 10,000 requests
Cache invalidation	$0.005 per invalidation

Cloud interconnect

Cloud interconnect is used to connect your in-house infrastructure to Google Cloud Platform. Cloud Interconnect provides us with Interconnect and Peering services, with Interconnect having a Dedicated Interconnect and IPsec. In Interconnect, your in-house infra is connected to GCP VPC dedicatedly. And IPsec on the other hand, connects your in-house infra with Cloud VPC using IPsec VPN. It provides direct access to RFC1918 IPs, with an SLA.

Now, in Peering Connection, we have Direct Peering and Carrier Peering. Direct Peering and Carrier gives you access to Google's public IP, but without an SLA.

When to use:

The following figure shows when to go for Direct Peering, Carrier Peering, Dedicated Interconnect, or IPsec VPN:

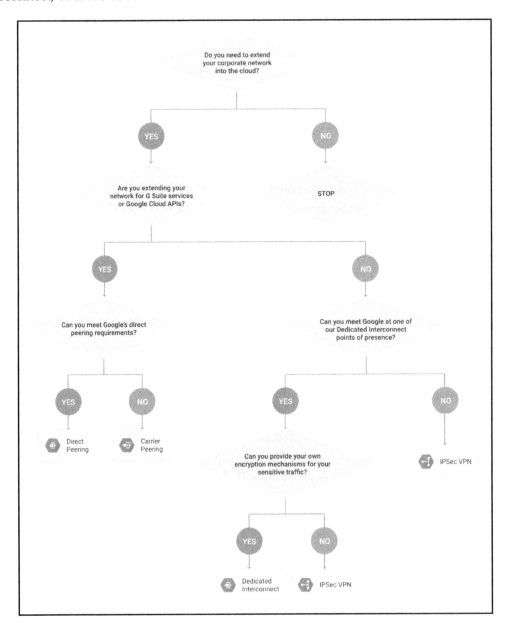

Costing:

Dedicated Interconnect:

To learn more about costing you can refer to the following link.

Dedicated Interconnect price: `https://cloud.google.com/interconnect/pricing`.

VPN:

Please refer to the following table for details about the costing of VPN:

Component billed	Price (USD)
Per tunnel (per hour)	$0.050
IPsec traffic	`https://cloud.google.com/compute/pricing#general`
Public IP for VPN Gateway	`https://cloud.google.com/compute/pricing#ipaddress`

Peering:

Please refer to the following table for details about the costing of Peering:

Pricing	Ingress	Intra-region google cloud platform traffic egress
Direct Peering	Free for all regions	• **NA:** $0.04/GB • **EU:** $0.05/GB • **APAC:** $0.06/GB
Carrier Peering	Free for all regions	• **NA:** $0.04/GB • **EU:** $0.05/GB • **APAC:** $0.06/GB

To learn more about costing, you can refer to the following link.

More pricing options: `https://cloud.google.com/interconnect/docs/how-to/carrier-peering`.

Cloud DNS

Cloud DNS is a reliable, resilient, and low-latency DNS to serve from Google's worldwide network. Cloud DNS is a scalable, reliable, and managed Domain Name Service using Google's infrastructure underlying. Mapping of IP addresses to web addresses is done using Cloud DNS.

When to use:

If you are building a website that requires hosting a domain name registry from Google, you can do that using Cloud DNS.

Special features:

- DNS Lookup: translates IPs into web addresses
- Good management: you can manage it through API and Web UI

Costing:

Please refer to the following table for details about the costing of Managed Zones:

Managed zones	Price
First 25 Managed Zones	$0.20 per managed zone per month
Managed Zones 26 through 10,000	$0.10 per managed zone per month
Managed Zones over 10,000	$0.03 per managed zone per month

Please refer to the following table for details about the costing of Query Traffic Costs:

Traffic	Price
First 1 billion queries	$0.40 per million queries per month
Queries over 1 billion	$0.20 per million queries per month

Network Service Tiers ALPHA

Network Service Tiers is in ALPHA stage. Using Network Service Tier, we can optimize a network with respect to performance or cost.

When to use:

Typically, network traffic hops multiple times before reaching the end user, using the best possible route to transmit data, but if we are willing to skip this and transmit data with least hops before reaching the end user we can use it.

Special features:

- High performance and reliability with global SLA and low latency
- Exceptional High Performing network

Big Data

Now we are going to discuss the services falling under the Big Data category:

- BigQuery
- Cloud Dataflow
- Cloud Dataproc
- Cloud Datalab
- Cloud Data prep BETA
- Cloud Pub/Sub
- Genomics
- Google Data Studio* BETA

We will discuss each of them in the following sections.

BigQuery

BigQuery is the data warehouse on Google Cloud Platform. It is cost-effective, fully managed, and works at scale.

When to use:

If you want to make your data work in a way to find some business insights, using SQL; also you do not need any database admin. While your data can be stored in cloud storage as an object or in Cloud SQL as a database, you can run your queries on the top of GCP using BigQuery.

Special features:

- Serverless
- Scale at Petabyte level
- Standard SQL on batch or real-time data
- Storage and Compute are priced differently

Costing:

Storage and computing are charged differently.

Please refer to the following table for details about the costing of BigQuery Storage:

Item	Price
Storage	$0.02 per GB, per month $0.01 per GB, per month for long term storage
Streaming Inserts	$0.01 per 200 MB
Loading, Copying, or Exporting Data Metadata Operations	Free

Please refer to the following table for details about the costing of BigQuery Compute:

FEATURE	PRICE
Pay-as-you-go	$5 per TB First terabyte (1TB) per month is free*
Flat-rate pricing	Starting at $40,000/month for a dedicated reservation of 2,000 slots.

Cloud Dataflow

The main purpose of Cloud Dataflow is to provide real-time transformation and enrich data. It also serves the purpose of reducing complexity. This is yet another component with serverless capabilities and is fully managed.

When to use:

If you want to build a pipeline where you transform data (real-time or batch) before subjecting it to Cloud Pub/Sub, BigQuery, or Machine Learning.

Special features:

- Auto scales horizontally
- Unified Programming Model
- Automated Resource Management

Costing:

Please refer to the following table for details about the costing of Cloud Dataflow for the Iowa region:

Cloud Dataflow Worker Type	vCPU $/hr	Memory $ GB/hr	Storage—Standard Persistent Disk $ GB/hr	Storage—SSD Persistent Disk $ GB/hr	Cloud Dataflow Shuffle $ GB/hr
Batch	$0.056	$0.003557	$0.000054	$0.000298	$0.0216
Streaming	$0.069	$0.003557	$0.000054	$0.000298	N/A

Cloud Dataproc

Cloud Dataproc provides us with the power of Hadoop and Spark. Using Cloud Dataproc, we can build our own Hadoop and Spark servers, with all the prominent services auto installed. Cloud Dataproc is well integrated with other GCP components.

When to use:

Cloud Dataproc can be used when you have an established application on Hadoop. But now as your data is growing and demand in resources is varying, you need features such as auto scaling, elastic load balancer, and no overhead of Hadoop Admin tasks—in such scenarios you can go with Cloud Dataproc.

Special features:

- Resizable cluster
- Automated cluster management
- Configurations automatic or manual
- Versioning helps you in changing versions in Hadoop and Spark

Costing:

Please refer to the following table for details about the costing of Cloud Dataproc, for the Iowa region:

Machine type	Price
Standard Machines 1-64 Virtual CPUs	$0.010—$0.640
High Memory Machines 2-64 Virtual CPUs	$0.020—$0.640
High CPU Machines 2-64 Virtual CPUs	$0.020—$0.640
Custom Machines Based on vCPU and memory usage	$0.010/ vCPU hour

Cloud Datalab

Cloud Dataproc is a very powerful exploration tool. Using Cloud Dataproc, we can explore, analyze, transform, and visualize data. Using this data, we can build our own Machine Learning models.

When to use:

Cloud Datalab being built on Jupyter and having great integration with BigQuery, Cloud Machine Learning Engine, Google Compute Engine, and Google Cloud Storage you can use Python. Along with Python you can also use SQL and JavaScript.

Special features:

- Supports Python, SQL, and JavaScript
- Supports Tensorflow-based deep Machine Learning
- Based on Jupyter, thus familiar for many
- Notebook format

Costing:

Data lab is free. You may incur compute, storage, and other cloud services costs based on usage.

Cloud Dataprep BETA

Cloud Dataprep is considered as a cloud data service to explore data visually, as well as prepare data for analysis. This service is in Beta right now. It is visually very interactive and easy to use.

When to use:

Major utility of Cloud Dataprep will be when you need to clean, explore, and prepare structured or unstructured data. But you also are not looking for any infrastructure deployment or managing it.

Special features:

- Automatically detects schemas, datatypes, joins, and anomalies, if any
- Fully managed
- Serverless
- Supports almost all common data sources

Costing:

In Cloud Dataprep, users define the data preparation rules by interacting with a sample of their data. Use of the application is free. Once a data preparation flow has been defined, the sample can be exported for free or the flow can be executed as a Cloud Dataprep job, which will incur charges.

Cloud Pub/Sub

Delivering real-time event driven data at any scale with reliability. Using Cloud Pub/Sub you can do stream analytics on real-time data.

When to use:

If the data is coming at a great pace and you want to collect the data and analyze it with respect to events. Cloud Pub/Sub can divert the data to Cloud Dataflow and it then can be transmitted to BigQuery for datawarehousing.

Special features: The following are the special features of Cloud Pub/Sub:

- Ensure at-least-one delivery
- Global by default
- Open APISs

Costing:

Please refer to the following table for details about the costing of Cloud Pub/Sub:

Monthly data volume	Price per GB
First 10GB	$0.00
Next 50TB	$0.06
Next 100TB	$0.05
Beyond 150TB	$0.04

Genomics

Genomics is used when you have to process huge amounts of genomics data.

When to use:

Earlier to process the genomics data it was costing huge and eventually was consuming good time in analyzing and processing. But now with the help of Genomics we can put VMs with huge computing power at work to get the output in seconds and at a minuscule cost.

Special features:

- Security and Compliance
- Real-time processing
- Interoperability

Costing:

Google Genomics charges for data storage. Loading and exporting genomic data is free of charge. Other cloud resources consumed while using Google Genomics are billed at the standard rates:

Resource	Cost (in US$)
Genomics storage*	$0.022/GB Per Month

Google Data Studio BETA

Google Data Studio is used to create better reports and more informative dashboards. These reports and dashboards are easy to share, easy to read, and are fully customizable.

When to use:

If you want to make a great presentation to propose some business insights to non-technical people. In such cases Google Data Studio can be the best option.

Special features:

The following are the special features of Google Data Studio:

- **Data Connections, Transformation, and Visualization**: you can connect Google Data Studio to some databases, transform the data using mathematical formulas, and then visualize it in the form of bar charts or pie charts
- **Administration:** You have the authority to decide access to the Google Data Studio with Google Drive kind of easy management
- **Sharing and Collaboration:** with the power of Google Docs, Sheets, and Slides you can collaborate and share the docs in real-time

Costing:

Google Data Studio is free to use.

Data transfer

In this section, we are going to discuss the services falling under the Data Transfer category:

- Google Transfer Appliance
- Cloud Storage Transfer Service
- Google BigQuery Data Transfer Service

We will discuss each of them in the following sections.

Google Transfer appliance

Google Transfer Appliance can be used to transfer data to Google Server offline.

When to use:

If you are migrating your complete data center, then data can exceed the petabyte scale. In this scenario, if you consider the available bandwidth of internet, it will be too costly and time consuming to upload data over the internet. Therefore, we use Google Transfer Appliance.

Special features:

- **Secure**: Data is encrypted
- **Uploads huge data**: 100 GB to 480 TB in a single appliance

Costing:

Please refer to the following table for details about the costing of Google Transfer appliance:

Transfer appliance option	Usage fee	Free days of onsite usage	Late fee per day, beyond allotment	Typical 2-day shipping fee
100 TB	$300	10	$30	$500
480 TB	$1800	25	$90	$900

Cloud Storage Transfer Service

Cloud Storage Transfer Service comes with two features – transferring data from other cloud provider's bucket (such as Amazon S3) and transferring data within different Google Cloud Platform.

When to use:

Consider you are part of a huge enterprise, and this enterprise is using different cloud vendors for different verticals. In such scenarios, it might so happen that the data the enterprise owns is on Amazon S3. But as you want the same data to be used for building some machine learning model, then you need that data with you.

Special features:

The following are the special features of Cloud Storage Transfer Service:

- **Single API**: provides a single API to access/copy/move data across storage
- **Highly durable**: 99. 999999999% durability

Costing:

To learn more about costing you can refer to the following link.

Costing of Cloud Storage Transfer Service, `https://cloud.google.com/storage/transfer/`
.

Google BigQuery Data Transfer Service

Google BigQuery Data Transfer Service helps us to import all the data that Google SaaS applications generate. Within a few clicks you will have the data of AdWords, DoubleClick campaign Manager, and many other applications.

When to use:

Suppose you just ran an ad campaign for a client. AdWords has its own set of parameters to show some analytical reports. But your client is looking for some more reports that AdWords does not provide by default. Then you can import this data into Google BigQuery using Google BigQuery Data Transfer Service for further analysis.

Special features:

The following are the special features of Google BigQuery Data Transfer Service:

- **Simple**: within a few clicks you can enable this service
- **Good connectivity**: it supports imports from AdWords, YouTube reports, and many more

Costing:

Please refer to the following table for details about the costing of Google Bigquery Data Transfer Service:

Source application	Monthly price (prorated)
Google AdWords	$2.50 per unique Customer ID—External Customer IDs in the Customer table, including zero impression Customer IDs.
DoubleClick Campaign Manager	$2.50 per unique Advertiser ID—Advertiser IDs in the impression table.
DoubleClick for Publishers	$100 per Network ID
YouTube	No charge through April 1, 2018. Pricing for YouTube to be announced at a later date.

Cloud AI

Now we are going to discuss the services falling under the Cloud AI category, such as:

- Cloud AutoML alpha
- Cloud TPU beta
- Cloud machine learning engine
- Cloud job discovery private beta
  Dialogflow Enterprise Edition Beta
- Cloud natural language
- Cloud Speech API, Translation API and Vision API
- Cloud Video Intelligence

We will discuss each of them in the following sections.

Cloud AutoML alpha

Cloud AutoML is in alpha stage right now. Cloud AutoML can be used to train high quality custom machine learning models in the simplest form possible.

It is the first product in AutoML Vision; using this, you can train custom vision models of our own.

Cloud TPU beta

Cloud TPU can be called an accelerated machine learning service. Cloud TPU uses Tensorflow to accelerate machine learning.

When to use:

Cloud TPU can be used for any general machine learning use case.

Special features:

The following are the special features of Cloud TPU Beta:

- **Supercomputing**: Cloud TPU provides you with supercomputing power for machine learning models
- **Easy to migrate**: Cloud TPU is well integrated with Tensorflow, thus making it easy to migrate

Costing:

There is no costing information as the service is in beta.

Cloud machine learning engine

Cloud Machine Learning Engine is the platform where you can build your own machine learning models. Using Tensorflow we can create our own model to execute on any kind of data at any scale.

It is well integrated with Google Cloud Dataflow for pre-pre-processing, thus accessing Google Cloud Storage and Google BigQuery.

When to use:

If you have huge data in Cloud Storage in text format and you want to build a machine learning model on the top of it, you can opt for Cloud machine learning.

Special features:

The following are the special features of Cloud machine learning engine:

- **Integrated**: works with Cloud Dataflow, Cloud storage, and Cloud Datalab
- **Scalable**: you can build a scalable cluster with many nodes

Costing:

To learn more about costing you can refer to the following link.

Costing for Cloud Machine Learning Engine: `https://cloud.google.com/ml-engine/pricing`.

Cloud job discovery private beta

Cloud Job Discovery is majorly used for hiring employees. It is very useful while improving your complete recruitment system.

When to use:

If you want to build a job recruitment platform where you want the features of auto spelling correction, concept recognition, and job enrichment.

Special features:

The following are the special features of Cloud Job Discovery Private Beta:

- **Integrated**: Cloud Job Discovery is integrated with Jibe, Ongig, and many more
- **Good conversion rate**: CJD increases the chances of a candidate being hired

Costing:

Costing information is not provided yet as the service is in private beta as of now.

Dialogflow enterprise edition beta

Dialogflow enterprise is in beta right now. Dialogflow is useful to have a machine learning application or bot on our website to help us with natural and rich interactions between users coming to the business—in short a chatbot.

When to use:

A travel website might receive repeated inquiries in terms of flight tickets, travel packages, hotel ratings, and many more. So, instead of allotting an actual human, we can use Dialogflow, which can help customers get the right information without any delay.

Special features:

- **Customer Service:** You can have an application that can perform tasks with respect to past orders, scheduling meetings, or helping users with typical requests
- **Commerce:** Using Dialogflow, you can let the user make an order through a chat window only

Costing:

Please refer to the following table for details about the costing of Dialogflow Enterprise Edition:

Features	Standard edition	Enterprise edition
Text Interaction	Free usage and unlimited requests	$0.002 per request
Voice Interaction	Up to 1,000 per day or a maximum of 15,000 per month	Unlimited pay-as-you-go at $0.0065 per request
Default Quota Limits for Voice	3 queries per second	10 queries per second
SLA	No	Coming soon (with GA release)
Support	Community support and via email	Eligible for Cloud Support packages with committed response times for supporting production applications

Cloud natural language

Cloud natural language can be used to build insights out of unstructured data such as messages, texts, tweets, blog spots, and so on.

When to use:

A company that is into digital marketing is serving a client who has a new food product being launched in the market and they want to know the response of the consumers. In that case, a digital marketing company can do sentimental analysis on the tweets or FB posts using cloud natural language.

Special features:

- **Sentimental analysis:** You can check the sentiments in a blog or set of text
- **Multi-language support**: Supports English, Spanish, Japanese, Italian, Korean, and many others
- **RESI API**: You can send your data directly to the REST API

Costing:

To learn more about costing, you can refer to the following link: `https://cloud.google.com/natural-language/pricing`.

Cloud speech API, translation API, and vision API

Cloud speech API converts speech to text using a powerful neural network. The translation API can be used to translate text from one language to another. And Vision API is used to identify an object in an image. All these are REST-based APIs.

When to use:

Speech API you can use when you want to build an application where you want to take audio inputs from the user. If you are building a website that might have viewers from all over the globe, but you cannot write for all of them, then you can use the translation API. And if you want to categorize images on the basis of location, you can use Vision API.

Special features:

The following are the special features of Speech API:

- **Speech**: Real-time and pre-recorded support: you can make use of Speech API for real-time as well as pre-recorded data
- **Better vocabulary**: Supports over 110 languages
- **Auto detection**: Language can be detected automatically on the basis of input

The following is the special feature of Translation API:

- **Text translation**: HTML data can be sent and received in some other language

The following is the special feature of Vision API:

- Avant-garde **visual features** help to detect inappropriate, vulgar, or adult content

Costing:

The costing for the Speech API is as follows:

Monthly usage	Price per 15 seconds
0—60 minutes	Free
61—1,000,000 minutes	$0.006

The costing for the translate API is as follows:

Feature	Cost (usd) up to 1,000 m characters/month
Text Translation	$20 per million characters
Language detection	$20 per million characters

For the costing of the Vision API, you can refer to: `https://cloud.google.com/vision/pricing`.

Cloud video intelligence

Cloud video intelligence is used to perform analysis on videos.

When to use:

Suppose you want to create a platform where travel bloggers are creating blogs, uploading photos, and uploading videos. And you have to make sure that videos uploaded automatically identify the locations and the objects; in this case we can create the tags for all videos to make video search easy.

Special features:

The following are the special features of Cloud Video Intelligence:

- **Detect entities**: you can detect objects automatically, such as mountains and flowers, in the video
- **Explicit content**: adult content can be detected using this service in the video

Costing:

Please refer to the following table for details about the costing of Cloud Video Intelligence:

Feature	First 1000 minutes	Minutes 1001-100,000
Label detection	Free	$0.10 / minute
Shot detection	Free	$0.05 / minute, or free with Label detection
SafeSearch detection	Free	$0.10 / minute

Internet of Things

The Clout IoT Core is a cloud category that falls under the Internet of Things. Let's now discuss this in detail.

Cloud IoT Core beta

Clout IoT Core is in beta stage right now. Cloud IoT helps us in collecting data from numerous devices spread across globe. You can then ingest this data into other GCP services.

When to use:

If you are having hundreds of IoT devices in a factory. And typically they are collected locally in a server and transmitted physically. In this case the best option is to connect all the devices to the gateway and then you can send that data to Google IoT Core.

Special features:

- **Role-level access**: you can apply role-level access control to all the devices thus controlling the access to each device
- **Security**: this is a very important feature for most enterprises; features such as TLS 1.2, CA signed certificate, and so on are part of the service
- **Global system**: this is a single global system where you can have heterogeneous architecture where a few devices can run on HTTP and a few on MQTT, but they are still part of the same ecosystem

Costing:

To learn more about costing you can refer to the following link.

Costing for Cloud IoT Core: `https://cloud.google.com/iot/pricing`.

Management tools

Now we are going to discuss the services falling under management tools:

- Stackdriver overview
- Monitoring, logging, error Reporting, Trace, Debugger
- Cloud deployment manager
- Cloud console
- Cloud shell
- Cloud console mobile app

We will discuss each of them in the following sections.

Stackdriver overview

Stackdriver is the service that helps us with monitoring, logging, error reporting, tracing, and debugging the application—that too across cloud vendors and hybrid ecosystems.

When to use:

When an application becomes more complex in terms of number of services, number of applications, number of cloud vendors, and you cannot rely on admins much.

Special features:

The following are the special features of Stackdriver Overview:

- **Integrations**: You can integrate Stackdriver with AWS and local data centers
- **Dashboard**: Get the complete list of all the services running; error, alerts, and diagnostics of all services in one place

Costing:

Google Stackdriver offers a Basic tier and a Premium tier. The Premium tier is priced at a flat rate of $8.00 per chargeable monitored resource per month, prorated hourly.

For the costing for Stackdriver, you can refer to: `https://cloud.google.com/stackdriver/pricing`.

Alerting	Basic email	Advanced all notifications
User-defined metrics (custom and log based metrics)	Zero allocated	500 time series per resource, 250 metrics descriptors per project

In addition, customers who would like to use logs or user-defined metrics beyond the allocated amount in the two tiers can pay for overage:

Usage	Overage charges (beyond the included amount)
Logs ingestion	$0.50/GB
User-defined metric (custom metrics or logs metrics)	$0.10/timeseries, $1/metric descriptor

Monitoring, logging, error reporting, trace, and debugger

Monitoring, logging, error reporting, trace, and debugger are all separate services in Google Cloud Platform. You can use all of them to perform all the respective tasks.

Monitoring you are going to use to identify uptime and overall health of the application.

Logging can be used to manage logs in real-time and further analysis.

Error reporting helps us in understanding, categorizing, and identifying errors in our applications.

To find performance bottlenecks in the application, we can use trace.

Debugger is often useful when we have to debug our code while the code is already on the production.

When to use:

If the application needs to be monitored, logged, traced, or needs error reporting and debugging—you can use it.

Special features:

The following are the special features:

- **Monitoring**: AWS and GCP integration, Dashboards, can build custom metrics
- **Logging**: perform analytics using BigQuery, retention of logs, searching logs
- **Error Reporting**: instant notification, real-time processing, link errors using issue tacker to issue, handy mobile application
- **Trace**: automatic analysis, automatic performance insight, easy setup
- **Debugger**: easy team collaboration, can integrate Trace with IDE

Costing:

Stackdriver monitoring:

Please refer to the following table for details about the costing of stackdriver monitoring.

Category	Basic	Premium
Price	Free	$8.00 per resource per month, prorated hourly.
Metrics	GCP metrics	Basic tier plus AWS metrics, Stackdriver Monitoring agent metrics; and custom and logs-based metrics.
Custom and logs-based metrics allotment	None	500 custom and logs-based metric time series per resource.
Custom and logs-based metrics allotment overage	$0.10 per time series per month	$0.10 per time series per month
Dashboards and Alerts	Custom dashboards and charts; Alerting with email notifications	Basic tier plus alerting with advanced notifications

Stackdriver logging and stackdriver error reporting:

Please refer to the following table for details about the costing of Stackdriver Logging and Stackdriver Error Reporting:

Feature	Basic tier	Premium tier
Price	Free	$8.001 per chargeable resource2 per month (prorated hourly)
Supported clouds	GCP only	GCP and AWS
Logs allotment3	50 GB per project per month	50 GB per project per month plus 14.25 MB per chargeable resource2 per hour
Logs retention: Admin activity audit logs Data access audit logs Non-audit logs	400 days 7 days 7 days	400 days 30 days 30 days
Metric data retention	6 weeks	6 weeks
Alerting policies	Some limitations	No limitations
Stackdriver Error Reporting, Stackdriver Debugger, and Stackdriver Trace	For applications on GCP	For applications on GCP and AWS (if supported)
Cloud Console Mobile App	Included	Included

Stackdriver trace and stackdriver debugger:

Trace and Debugger is free for all GCP customers.

Cloud deployment manager

Cloud deployment manager is used to create and manage templates for cloud resources with simple templates. We have to write that template in YAML format. Using Cloud Deployment Manager, we can deploy infrastructure that requires repeated efforts.

When to use:

If your application requires some resources for just three hours, but on a repeated basis; such as every week. In that case, instead of using a web console of GCP to start and stop these resources every week, you can write your own template in a declarative style (YAML).

Special features:

The following are the special features of Cloud Deployment Manager:

- **Parallel deployment**: you can deploy many infrastructure services in one go
- **Preview mode**: it helps you to get an idea of changes that your deployment is going to affect on your infrastructure

Costing:

Deployment manager is free to use for GCP customers.

Cloud console

Cloud console is the web UI that you can use to control the complete Google Cloud Platform.

When to use:

This will be used every time you want to use, web UI.

Special features:

The following are the special features of Cloud Console:

- **Resource management**: you can check status and health of all the resources at one place
- **SSH browser**: you can use this interface to log in easily into a VM instance
- **DevOps integration**: using a mobile app, you can very easily perform your DevOps tasks

Costing:

Cloud console is free to use for GCP customers.

Cloud shell

Cloud shell helps us in managing infrastructure using Command Prompt. You can access it using cloud console web UI.

When to use:

To access the complete GCP using CLI, you can use Cloud Shell.

Special features:

The following are the special features of Cloud Shell:

- **Browser access**: Can access Cloud Shell from a web browser
- **Secure**: Pre-authorized admin tool

Costing:

Cloud shell is free to use for GCP customers.

Cloud console mobile app

Cloud console mobile is the Android version of web-based cloud console.

Developer tools

Lastly, we are going to discuss the services falling under developer tools:

- Cloud SDK
- Container registry
- Container builder
- Cloud source repositories
- Cloud tools for IntelliJ, Visual Studio, Eclipse
- Cloud tools for Powershell

Let's learn about each of them in the following sections.

Cloud SDK

Cloud SDK is a set of tools that you can use in GCP on the command line, such as gcloud, gsutil, and bq. Using these tools we can access BigQuery, Google Cloud Compute Engine, Google Cloud Storage, and many more.

When to use:

You can use Cloud SDK to execute infrastructure services through the Command Prompt.

Special features:

The following are the special features of Cloud SDK:

- **Support gcloud, gsutil, bq:** Can access Cloud Platform APIs, Cloud Storage buckets/objects, and you can query and manipulate data though the Command Prompt
- **cmdlets**: Can access GCP tools from Windows environments

Costing:

Cloud SDK is free to use for GCP customers.

Container Registry

Container Registry can help us have fast and private Docker image storage on GCP.

When to use:

You can use Container Registry to store your private Docker images, and can do fast and scalable retrieval and deployment.

Special features:

The following are the special features of Container Register:

- **Kubernetes Engine**: can use Kubernetes Engine without any authentication setup
- **Regional Repositories**: you can store an image at the geographically closest location

Costing:

The Google Container Registry only charges for the Google Cloud Storage and network egress consumed by your Docker images.

Costing of the services: `https://cloud.google.com/container-registry/pricing`.

Container builder

Container builder can help us to build a container image in a fast, consistent, and trustworthy environment. You can build it in any language and package build artifacts into Docker.

When to use:

Container builder can be used to have a private and secure **Continuous Integration and Continuous Deployment (CI-CD)** on Google Cloud Platform.

Special features:

- **Integrate with IDE**: Container Builder can easily be integrated with existing IDE for CI-CD
- **Build and package**: We can build our source and package build artifacts into Docker container
- **History**: You get the complete history of all the build done so far for a specific cloud project

Costing:

Please refer to the following table for details about the costing of Container Builder:

Feature	Pricing
First 120 build-minutes per day	Free
Additional build-minutes	$0.0034 / minute

Cloud source repositories

Cloud source repositories are private Git repositories hosted on GCP. Source repositories provides Git version control to support collaborative development of any application or service, including those that run on app engine and Compute Engine.

When to use:

If, while using GCP, you require the repositories to store your code while working in collaboration, you can opt to go for cloud source repositories.

Special features:

- **Google hosted repos**: repos on GCP are completely private repos
- **Conected repos**: GCP repos are well connected with GitHub as well as BitBucket

Costing:

Please refer to the following table for details about the costing of cloud source repositories:

Free tier	Overages
Up to 5 Users	$1 per project-user over five project-users per month
50 GB Storage	$0.10 per GB storage per month
50 GB Egress	$0.10 per GB egress per month

Cloud tools for IntelliJ, Visual Studio, and Eclipse

Google Cloud Platform can help us to connect to various IDE tools, which includes IntelliJ, Visual Studio, and Eclipse. Using IntelliJ, we can deploy Java backend for a cloud app on Google App engine. Visual Studio integration can help us to build our ASP.NET programs seamlessly and deploy them at the same time.

For Eclipse, you need to use an open source plugin provided by GCP.

When to use:

Preferably when your team is working on GCP and native IDE is any of IntelliJ, Visual Studio, or Eclipse.

Special features:

The following are the special features:

- **IntelliJ**: App engine deployment for IntelliJ can interact with Cloud Source Repository hosted on GCP
- **Visual Studio**: Deploys an app directly onto Virtual Machines running IIS and ASP.NET and supports the latest version of Visual Studio VS 2015 and VS 2017

Costing:

Cloud Tools for IntelliJ, Visual Studio, Eclipse are not charged in Google Cloud Platform.

Cloud tools for Powershell

Cloud tools can help us have full control over a cloud using Windows PowerShell.

When to use:

Powershell is used to script, automate, and manage our Windows workloads running on Cloud Platform. Being familiar with Powershell is a huge plus.

Special features:

The following are the special features of Cloud Tools for Powershell:

- **Manage cloud storage:** You can upload/download from Cloud Storage or update ACLs
- **Deploy VMs:** Deployment of VMs in Compute Engine becomes easier

Costing:

Cloud Tools for Powershell is not charged in Google Cloud Platform.

Overview to Google Cloud Platform Console—Video

To get the complete overview of the GCP console and different features it offers click in link below or scan QR code.

Link: https://www.youtube.com/watch?v=Pq7QDkbiEqg

QR code:

Summary

In this chapter, we have understood all the services that Google Cloud Platform has to offer us. We have now got a complete idea of the different categories of all the services and how they are divided.

Along with that, we also have seen use cases that we can use those services in and an overview of the features each service has to provide.

In the next chapter, we are going to dive deep into services and tools surrounding ingestion and storing data.

4
Ingestion and Storing – Bring the Data and Capture It

Hello techies! So this is our first chapter in which we are going to delve into understanding the major services involving ingestion and storing. We have multiple options associated with ingestion and storage. Let's discuss the most important of them. They are given as the following:

- Cloud Dataflow
- Cloud Pub/Sub
- Cloud storage
- Cloud SQL
- Cloud BigTable
- Cloud Spanner
- Cloud Datastore
- Persistent disks

Cloud Dataflow

Cloud Dataflow is one of the first services we are going to learn in this chapter. It is a fully managed service that transforms data in the streams and batches while providing equal reliability.

You can develop a simplified and fast pipeline in Cloud Dataflow. We can express Cloud Dataflow in Java and the Python API in the Apache Beam SDK.

When to use

We have multiple uses of the Cloud Dataflow service in Google Cloud Platform.

We can use it for clickstream, point-of-sale, and segmentation analysis in retail. Cloud Dataflow can help the company getting the data to analyze it on the go and take important business decisions.

Another use case can be fraud detection in financial services. We can have Cloud Pub/Sub helping in gathering data from multiple data sources, which can increase the efficiency of fraud detection and accuracy.

You can also use Dataflow to provide personalized user experience in gaming to millions of users depending on their behavior.

IoT also generates huge data. And providing this data with analytics can be a huge plus. Logistics, healthcare, and manufacturing are a few of the sectors in IoT that Dataflow can address.

Special features

Cloud Dataflow comes with a Unified Programming Model, offering MapReduce-like operations through Apache Beam. We have very powerful data windowing and fine-grained correctness control for streaming and batch data. This makes Cloud Dataflow a very strong service in GCP.

When working with Cloud Dataflow, other aspects before choosing it can be the capacity of Dataflow to handle fault-tolerant execution with consistency and correctness irrespective of data size, cluster size, processing pattern, or pipeline complexity.

We can also integrate Dataflow with Stackdriver, GCP's unified logging, error reporting, debugging, and monitoring solutions, therefore allowing monitoring and troubleshooting pipelines on the go.

We can also integrate TensorFlow-based Cloud Machine Learning models into Dataflow. Multiple ML APIs are also supported on your data processing pipeline.

It integrates very well with the following streaming-based services:

- Cloud Pub/Sub
- BigQuery
- Cloud Machine Learning

- Cloud Datastore
- Apache Kafka
- Apache Avro

The placement for Cloud Dataflow is illustrated in the following image:

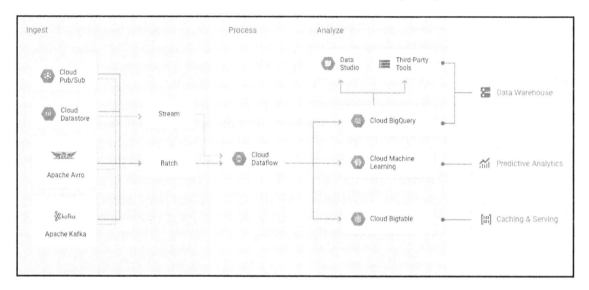

The Dataflow programming model

Cloud Dataflow runner services execute various data processing jobs that are created using the Dataflow SDK in a programming model that simplifies large-scale data processing.

We have our code programming model divided in four major components:

- **Pipelines**: Represents a single, repeatable job from start to finish
- **PCollections**: Represents a set of data in your pipeline
- **Transforms**: Performs processing on the elements of PCollection
- **I/O Sources and Sinks**: Provides data source / data sink APIs for pipeline I/O

Let's discuss them one by one in the following topics.

Pipelines

Pipelines in Cloud Dataflow represent a data processing job, encapsulating entire series of computations. A pipeline supports input data from multiple external sources, is capable of transforming the data, and writes output data. Output data is typically written to an external data sink, which can be one of many GCP Data Storage services.

Dataflow can easily convert data from one format to another. A pipeline is built by writing a program using the Dataflow SDK.

Pipelines consists of two parts:

- **Data**: Specialized collection classes called PCollection
- **Transforms**: A step in your pipeline or a data processing operation

PCollection (data)

We have two PCollection classes: specialized container classes and representing datasets of virtually unlimited size. A PCollection represents a pipeline's input, intermediate, and output data while supporting parallelized processing.

PCollections need to be created for any data to be worked upon. At the same time, we also have to understand that PCollections are immutable; that is, the elements of an existing PCollection cannot be changed. They also don't support random access to individual elements. Every individual element belongs to a pipeline in which it is created. Hence, it cannot be shared between the pipeline objects. One PCollection can be generated from another PCollection after computation. We have a size factor associated with PCollection as well. They can be bounded or unbounded as determined at the time of creation.

- Bounded PCollection:
    - Represents a fixed dataset (known size; the size doesn't change)
    - g. server logs for a particular month
    - TextIO and BigQueryIO (root transforms) create a bounded PCollection
    - Can be processed using batch jobs
- Unbounded PCollection:
    - Represents a continuously updating dataset or streaming data
    - g. server logs as they are generated

- PubsubIO (root transforms) creates an unbounded PCollection
- Requires a concept called *windowing* to divide continuous updating data into logical windows of fixed size

Every collection in a PCollection contains a timestamp, and this timestamp is very helpful while working with windowing. Windowing is most useful with an unbounded PCollection. Timestamps present in each element in a PCollection are used for Windowing. Windowing helps us in dividing elements according to their timestamps. We can also assign our own timestamps to each element.

There can be different kinds of windows to divide the elements:

- Fixed time windows
- Sliding time windows
- Per-session windows
- Single global window

Transforms

Transforms is a step in the pipeline or a data processing operation. One or more PCollections can be treated as input to the Transforms, and the end result is another PCollection as an output. We might have a branching pipeline or a pipeline with a repeated structure while being able to use conditionals, loops, and so on.

First we will understand core transforms, then composite transforms, and at the end, root transforms.

Core transforms represent basic or common processing operations that we might require to perform on the data. We pass processing logic as a function object, and this function is applied to the element that we receive as an input PCollection. We can have this function object on multiple Google Compute Engines.

The function object must be serializable. It must be thread compatible, although Dataflow SDKs are not thread-safe. The function should always provide the same output. The following are the core transforms:

- **ParDo**: For generic parallel processing
- **GroupByKey**: For key-grouping key/value pairs
- **Combine**: For combining collections or grouped values
- **Flatten**: For merging collections

The next type is composite transforms. Composite transforms combine multiple transforms and are built from multiple sub-transforms. Averaging/summing numerical data, Map/Reduce style processing, and statistical analysis are a few of the applications they are expected to perform.

The third and final type of transform is root transforms. Root transforms are used at the start of a pipeline. It creates an initial PCollection. They include read transforms, write transforms, and create transforms:

- **Read transform**: Can serve as a root of the pipeline
- **Write transform**: Can serve as pipeline endpoints
- **Create transform**: Useful for creating a PCollection from in-memory data

I/O sources and sinks

The last part of Dataflow's programming model is I/O Sources and Sinks. Source APIs read data into the pipeline whereas sink APIs write output data from the pipeline.

Source and sink operations represent roots and endpoints of your pipeline. We can also create a custom data source and sink:

- **Read transform**: Reads data from external data source and returns a PCollection
- **Write transform**: Writes data in a PCollection to an external data source

Pipeline example

The following example is written in Java and shows constructing and running a pipeline with three transforms; they are:

- Transform to read
- Transform to count the data
- Transform to write out the results of the data

The code for the same is as follows:

```
public static void main(String[] args) {
        // create a pipeline parameterized by command-line flags
        PipelineOptions options =
PipelineOptionsFactory.fromArgs(args);
        Pipeline p = Pipeline.create(options);
        p.apply(TextIO.Read.from("gs://..."))          // read
```

```
input
        p.apply(new CountWords())                              // do
processing
        p.apply(TextIO.Write.to("gs://..."));                  // write
output
        p.run();                                               // run the
pipeline
}
```

How to use Cloud Dataflow - Video

Below is the video that will explain you how to use this service.

Link: https://www.youtube.com/watch?v=x0fvM1B2axI

QR code:

Cloud Pub/Sub

It is a message-oriented middleware to the cloud that is simple and provides scalability, flexibility, and reliability for streaming analytics and event-driven computing systems.

It provides many-to-many asynchronous messaging, decoupling senders and receivers. It allows secure and highly available communication between independently written applications. The following image shows the architecture of Cloud Pub/Sub:

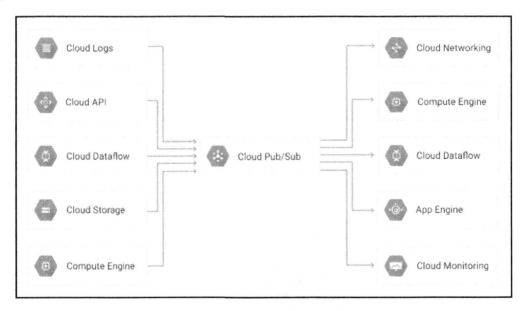

When to use

The following table illustrates some of the use cases for Google Pub/Sub:

Balancing workloads in a network cluster	Efficiently distributing a large queue of tasks among multiple workers, like GCE
Implementing asynchronous workflows	An order processing application can place an order on a topic, from where it can be picked/processed by one or more worker
Distributing event notifications	A service sends notification on new user registration. Subscriber will receive the notification after registration completion.
Refreshing distributed caches	An application can publish invalidation events to update the IDs of objects that have changed

Logging to multiple systems	GCE can write logs to multiple systems such as databases and monitoring systems so that they can be queried later
Data streaming from various processes or devices	Data can be streamed from different devices into the backend host
Reliability improvement	GCE can operate in additional zones by subscribing to a topic

Special feature

Google Cloud Pub/Sub is a publish/subscribe service and a real-time messaging service. It allows you to send and receive messages between applications asynchronously, at the same time providing a reliable and persistent queue. Using application-level acknowledgement, it increases reliability.

Undelivered data can be retained for as many as 7 days. Sharding, replication, load-balancing, and partitioning of the incoming data is automatically managed for streaming data.

Without any requirement for pre-provisioning of resources, it scales quickly and automatically to meet the demand. In the below diagram we can see that how Cloud Pub/Sub is part of the ingest strategy in GCP architecture. It is receiving data from multiple applications, devices and databases.

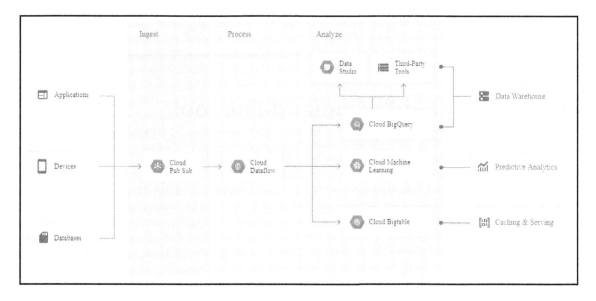

Overview

This messaging service is where the senders of messages are decoupled from the receivers of messages. There are several key concepts in a Pub/Sub service:

- **Message**: The data that moves through the service.
- **Topic**: A named entity that represents a feed of messages.
- **Subscription**: A named entity that represents an interest in receiving messages on a particular topic.
- **Publisher**: Also called a producer. It creates messages and sends/publishes them to the messaging service on a specified topic.
- **Subscriber**: Also called a consumer. It receives messages on the specified subscription.

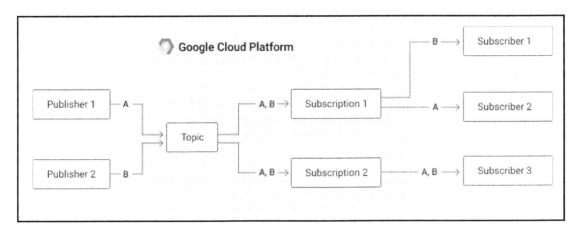

Using the gcloud command-line tool

The gcloud command-line tool is included in the Cloud SDK. This tool is used to perform operations in Cloud Pub/Sub. As we can see in the following program, first we are creating a topic with the name myTopic. Then we are creating a subscription mySubscription and assigning it to myTopic. Once this is done we are sending data or publishing data to the topic, myTopic with the message Hello World!!.

And the last thing that we are doing is to pull the subscription to receive the data. You can also use push subscription.

```
gcloud init
gcloud pubsub topics create myTopic
gcloud pubsub subscriptions create --topic myTopic mySubscription
gcloud pubsub topics publish myTopic --message "Hello World !!!"
gcloud pubsub subscriptions pull --auto-ack mySubscription
```

How to use Cloud Pub Sub - Video

Below is the video that will explain you how to use this service.

Link: https://www.youtube.com/watch?v=QSH37dlt8G4

QR code:

Cloud storage

Cloud Storage is a service in GCP whereby we can store any kind of data format in the form of unified object storage. It serves the highly useful purpose of storing data for enterprises and developers. We can use Cloud Storage for storing real-time data as well as archiving data.

We are provided with multiple storage options in Cloud Storage. Let's first understand the major benefits of Cloud Storage.

When to use it

We can use Cloud Storage for storing media content and storage delivery. We can also have data backups and archive data storage in terms of retrieval frequency and total duration.

Cloud Storage can also be treated as an integrated repository for analytics and machine learning. Along with this, we can store our huge videos and music content on Cloud Storage, which can be streamed. Storing images and website content would be very simple to think of, but it can be very cost effective.

We can use Cloud Storage for video transcoding as well, where we can have Cloud Storage as source of the data. The customer can access this data, which will be processed by a transcoder as per the customer's requirement.

Other uses can be to archive or tape migrations and disaster recovery.

Special feature

Cloud Storage is an object storage. But what exactly is Object Storage? Object storage organizes information into flexi-size containers called as objects, and these objects are our files of any extension. Every object (or file in our terms) comprises data and its metadata. Every object needs to have a globally unique name. Data is stored as separate objects and not placed in any hierarchy of directories, like what we have in the Windows OS.

Object storage uses two ways to protect the data:

- **Replication**: Stores multiple copies of each object on different nodes.
- **Erasure coding**: This divides an object into multiple pieces and calculates multiple parities. Parity is a technique that checks whether data has been lost or overwritten when it is moved from one place in storage to another.

The distributed nature of object storage enables two characteristics:

- **Shared-nothing architecture**: This combines independent and autonomous nodes into a federated data store. None of the nodes share the disk storage or memory. Unlike block storage, which can only be accessed when attached to an OS, object storage can be accessed through APIs or http/https.
- **Parallel tasks**: A large number of tasks run in parallel.

We have Cloud Storage scalable to exabytes of data. It also offers unlimited object storage (as long as you have money to pay for that), supporting a maximum single file size of 5 TB. Cloud Storage is designed for 99.999999999% (eleven 9's) durability as it stores data redundantly with automatic checksums to ensure data integrity. Cloud storage also provides high availability across all storage classes. We have a single API across storage classes, simplifying things.

Using Cloud Storage, we can move from one cloud to another cloud. We can use the Cloud Storage Transfer Service for this purpose. We can transfer data from one online data source to Google cloud storage; for example, the data source can be an Amazon S3 bucket, an http/https location, or a GCS bucket.

The second option is move from on-premise to cloud using a transfer appliance. It is a rackable, high-performance storage server. This appliance can be connected to an on-premise location, and you can fill it with your data. And then it is shipped to GCP region location where the data is uploaded to GCS. The storage capacity of this appliance can be between 100TB and 480TB.

Cloud storage classes

Every bucket that we create in cloud storage has three major properties.

- Every bucket must have a global unique name.
- Every bucket will have content stored in the region to which the bucket belongs.
- And the last is the storage class of a bucket. It is standard by default.

We have four different storage classes:

- Multi-regional storage
- Regional storage
- Nearline storage
- Coldline storage

All storage classes have the same throughput and low latency (time to the first byte, typically tens of milliseconds).

All storage classes will be using the same tools and APIs to access data (such as *gsutil* and *GCP Console),* same OAuth, and same granular access controls to secure your data. There will be no minimum object size and pay-for-use model.

We have many other features such as object versioning, object notification, access logging, life cycle management and so on in Cloud Storage.

Now we will be discussing different storage classes offered by Cloud Storage.

Multi-regional storage

Multi-regional storage is suitable for storing data that is frequently accessed, also termed as **hot objects**. Examples are serving website content, interactive workloads, data supporting mobiles, and gaming applications. High availability is a major plus point compared to other storage classes.

Multi-Regional storage, as the name suggests, is a geo-redundant storage class. That means it stores data redundantly in at least two geographic places that are at least 100 miles apart. Geo-redundancy occurs asynchronously.

One thing that you must be aware of is that data can be placed only in multi-regional locations such as Asia, EU, and US, and not like regional locations like asia-south1, us-west1 and so on.

Regional storage

In regional storage, data storage capacity is low. It brings the constraint that data can be placed/stored only in a regional location. It is suitable to store data in the same regional location as GCE or Kubernetes Engine clusters that use the data.

Nearline storage

Nearline and Coldline are two different storage classes for archiving data. Due to these, it is a low-cost and highly durable storage service. You can store the data that is infrequently accessed.

The availability for this storage is slightly lower than for regional or multi-regional storage. Nearline comes with a minimum 30-day storage duration, which means you can access the data within 30 days but you have to pay for the 30-day duration.

Its use is good for data that you plan to read/update merely once a month. It is more suitable for data backup, disaster recovery, and archival storage.

Coldline storage

Coldline is another storage type for archival data. It is a very cheap and highly durable storage service. it is mainly used for data archiving, online backup, and disaster recovery.

Data is available in milliseconds of latency. The major difference between coldline storage and nearline storage is that data in coldline is better accessed at most once a year, due to slightly lower availability. Minimum storage duration is 90-day, that means minimum you will be charged for 90 days of coldline storage.

Standard storage

And finally, we have a default storage class listed as standard storage. It is more like multi-regional storage when the associated bucket is in a multi-regional location. But it is equivalent to regional storage when the associated bucket is in a regional location.

For example:

- A standard storage object is in multi-regional location, let's say, us
- In the console, object appears as multi-regional storage
- In the API, object appears as standard storage

Working with storages

The following code can be used to create storage buckets:

```
gsutil mb -p [PROJECT_NAME] -c [STORAGE_CLASS] -l [BUCKET_LOCATION]
gs://[BUCKET_NAME]/
```

Listing buckets in a project can be done using this code:

```
gsutil ls
```

We will use the following code to get bucket information or listing a buckets contents:

```
gsutil ls -r gs://[BUCKET_NAME]/**
```

The following code is used to copy files from your old bucket to your new bucket:

```
gsutil cp -r gs://[SOURCE_BUCKET]/* gs://[DESTINATION_BUCKET]
```

We can use the following code to delete the files from the bucket:

```
gsutil rm -r gs://[BUCKET_NAME]/**
```

We will use this code to delete the bucket and the files in the bucket:

```
gsutil ls -r gs://[BUCKET_NAME]
```

How to use Cloud Storage - Video

Below is the video that will explain you how to use this service.

Link: https://www.youtube.com/watch?v=owygBVd9PnU

QR code:

Cloud SQL

Cloud SQL is a fully managed database service that makes it easy to work with relational MySQL and PostgreSQL databases in the cloud. For now, we have few options in Cloud SQL. They offer high performance, scalability, and convenience.

When to use

Cloud SQL is very simple to use and has fixed use cases. It is used as a database infrastructure for applications running elsewhere.

You can also use it for wordpress sites, e-commerce applications, CRM tools, and geospatial applications that are compatible with MySQL or PostgreSQL. Thus, in the use cases where you might have to opt for MySQL or PostgreSQL, you can opt for Cloud SQL.

Special feature

Cloud SQL comes with great features like... using it is very easy. You don't require any software installation. We have backups, replication, patches, and updates' automation, thus leaving less headache! The availability as much as 99.95%.

It provides 10 TB of storage capacity, 40,000 IOPS, and 416 GB of RAM per instance while delivering high performance and scalability at the same time. It is very cost effective due to its offering of per-second billing. GCP is not going to ask for any commitment, but the longer you stay, the more sustained are the discounts offered.

It is easy to start and stop database instances, with auto data encryption.

We have two database engines: MySQL and PostgreSQL. Let's discuss on both of them.

Database engine (MySQL)

Cloud SQL provisions fully managed MySQL community edition databases. In the cloud of 2nd generation instance, it support MySQL 5.6 and 5.7. As we already know, the instance can provide as much as 416 GB of RAM and 10 TB of storage; and that is huge.

If you allotted less storage while provisioning and after few months you have a requirement of increasing the storage, you are free to do that.

Cloud SQL also supports first generation MySQL 5.5 and 5.6 but provides limited instance types of up to 16 GB of RAM and 500 GB of storage. Cloud SQL has regions covered in USA, EU, and Asia.

Encryption is also done on the customer's data in Google's internal networks, database tables, temporary files, and backups. You can also use mysqldump to import and export databases. Or simply import and export CSV files.

There is support for secure external connections with Cloud SQL proxy (SSL protocol), instance cloning, and integration with stackdriver logging and monitoring.

Database engine (PostgreSQL)

Then we have this second option in Cloud SQL, which is also a fully managed PostgreSQL 9.6 database in the cloud, where you can store data up to 10 TB in size.

Most other features of PostgreSQL are similar to MySQL. Like, you have the option to increase the storage when needed; USA, EU, and Asia regions are supported; and so on.

Encryption, backups, importing and exporting of data using SQL dump files, support for secure external connection with Cloud SQL, and integration with Stackdriver logging and monitoring are a few of the other major features.

How to use Cloud SQL - Video

Below is the video that will explain you how to use this service.

Link: `https://www.youtube.com/watch?v=D7mWwMveLfk`

QR code:

Cloud BigTable

Cloud BigTable is a high-performance NoSQL database service for large analytical and operational workloads. BigTable is a sparse, distributed, persistent, and multi-dimensional sorted map. The map is indexed by a row key, column key, and a timestamp.

When to use it

Cloud BigTable is used mainly for large-scale, low-latency applications; throughput-intensive data processing; and analytics.

We can also use Cloud BigTable to store very large amounts of single-keyed data with very low latency.

Special features

Cloud BigTable is designed to handle massive workloads at consistent low latency and high read-write throughput. For IoT, user analytics, and financial data analysis, it is also a great choice for operational and analytical application.

It is a petabyte-scale service and can be easily integrated with Hadoop, GCP Dataflow, and GCP Dataproc. Apache HBase and Cloud BigTable support open-source industry standard HBase API.

Encryption of data is done in both ways: in flight and at rest.

Cloud BigTable storage model

Cloud BigTable stores massively scalable tables, while each table is a sorted key/value map.

Table rows are described as a single entity and table columns contain individual values for each row.

The following is the table structure you can refer to:

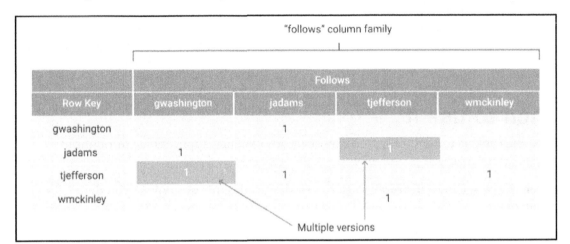

Each row in Cloud BigTable is indexed by a single row key; or we can say a single value in each row is indexed. This value is called the row key. This row key can be a unique identifier.

And each column is identified by a combination of column-family and column-qualifier. Here, column-qualifier is a unique name within the column-family. One column-family can contain multiple column-qualifiers, while column-qualifiers are used as data.

Cloud Bigtable architecture

Now we will be studying the Cloud BigTable architecture. When we make a request, all the requests will go through a frontend server before they are sent to a cloud bigtable node.

These nodes are then organized into a Cloud Bigtable Cluster. This Cloud Bigtable Cluster belongs to the Cloud Bigtable instance, which is a container for the cluster. Every node in the cluster handles a subset of requests to the cluster made by the client.

If you are willing to utilize the maximum throughput of the cluster and a number of simultaneous requests, then adding nodes is a good option:

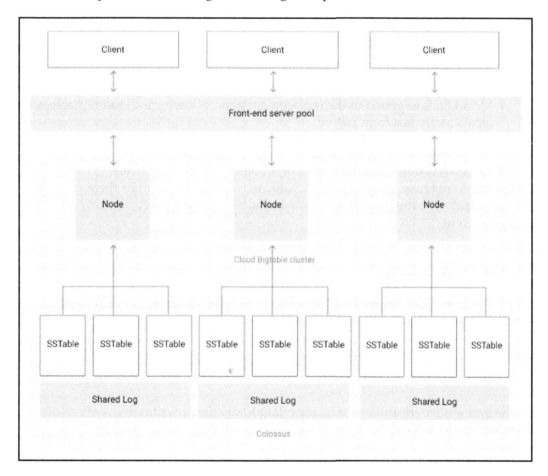

Just like we have Apache HBase sharded into blocks of continuous rows called tablets, Cloud BigTable also has the same architecture. Sharding is done to balance the query workload and tablets are stored on Colossus. Colossus is Google's filesystem in SSTable format; this is a different topic to study altogether.

The purpose of SSTable is to provide a persistent, ordered, and immutable map from keys to values. Each tablet is associated with a Cloud Bigtable node.

Durability in the Cloud BigTable is provided by storing all writes in SSTable files, but data is never stored on Cloud BigTable nodes. Each node has pointers to a set of tablets that are stored on Colossus.

Advantages of using this architecture:

- As the actual data is not copied, rebalancing tablets from one node to another is very fast. Cloud BigTable simply updates the pointers for each node.
- Metadata is migrated to the replacement node, allowing a Cloud Bigtable node to recover very fast from failure.
- The best part is that there is no data loss when a Cloud Bigtable node fails.

Also, if your data has some missing values or, in other words, empty cells in Cloud Bigtable, they do not take up any space. A value to each key needs to be there to make it visible in the table. If a row does not include a value for a specific key, the key/value entry is simply not present.

Load balancing

The Master process manages the Cloud Bigtable zone. The same master also manages the workload and data volume within the clusters.

The master has the authority to split larger tablets (or more utilized tablets) in half, and merges smaller tablets (or less-accessed tablets) while redistributing them between the nodes.

To get the best write performance, it is important to distribute writes as evenly as possible across nodes.

How to use Cloud Bigtable—Video

Below is the video that will explain you how to use this service.

Link: https://www.youtube.com/watch?v=DvVfaH10BvQ

QR code:

Cloud Spanner

Now we are on the sixth topic: Cloud Spanner. Cloud Spanner is a fully managed, mission-critical, and relational database service that offers transactional consistency at a global scale, schemas, SQL, and automatic synchronous replication for high availability.

Cloud Spanner offers:

- Strong consistency
- SQL support
- Managed instances with high availability through transparent, synchronous, and built-in data replication
- Regional and multi-regional instance configurations

When to use

Cloud Spanner is ideal for relational, structured, and semi-structured data that requires high availability, strong consistency, and transactional reads and writes. In most cases, Cloud SQL would suffice your requirement, but Cloud Spanner can be a real savior when we are talking about consistency and high availability.

Special features

Cloud Spanner comes with great features. Transaction consistency and enterprise grade security top the list of those features. It is really a very highly available service, so we have to worry much less about any downtime. Plus it is fully managed, so even managing the service is not a concern for us.

Cloud Spanner supports many programming languages such as C#, Go, Java, Node.js, PHP, Python, and Ruby, and you can scale this service globally.

You also have all the features that any relational semantics would provide: schemas, ACID transactions, and support for SQL queries.

Schema and data model

The schema and data model of Cloud Spanner is very much similar to any normal RDBMS. Like, it has a database, and the database might contain one or more tables. A table's structure is also very much like RDBMS tables, where we have rows, columns, values, and primary keys.

Giving way to the data-locality relationship between the two independent tables, we can also define a parent-child relationship between the tables for efficient retrieval. Just like an RDBMS, each table mandatorily must have a primary key, and the primary key can be composed of zero or more columns.

The primary key column(s) of the primary table must be the prefix of the primary key of the child table in the parent-child table. The primary key of each of the child tables must be composed of the same N columns as in the parent table's primary key.

We have something called database splits as well in Cloud Spanner. Cloud Spanner divides your data into chunks called **splits**, where individual splits can move independently of each other.

A split is a range of rows in a top-level or non-interleaved table. An insertion of child rows between the parent rows along the primary key dimension is known as interleaving. The child tables are called interleaved tables, whereas split boundaries are the start and end keys of the split. Cloud Spanner automatically adds or removes the split boundaries, which changes the number of splits in the database.

Based on the load Cloud Spanner splits, the split boundaries are later added automatically when it detects high read or write loads spread among many keys in a split. Rows of an interleaved table cannot be split from their corresponding row in the parent table.

The parent-child relationship in the table gives you control over how data is sharded under the hood.

Instances

An instance needs to be created first within a GCP project to use Cloud Spanner. It is an allocation of resources that is used by Cloud Spanner databases created in that instance.

Instance creation includes two important choices:

- The instance configuration
- The node count

These choices determine the location and number of instances serving and storage resources. We have a provision for changing the node count, but this configuration choice is permanent for an instance.

The geographic placement is defined by instance configuration and the replication of the databases in that instance. Depending on whether resources are contained in a single GCP region or they span more than one region, instances can be regional or multi-regional.

Each node count provides up to 2 TB of storage, as Cloud Spanner nodes are dedicated resources. These nodes do background work to optimize and protect your data even when you are not running any workload.

How to use Cloud Spanner - Video

Below is the video that will explain you how to use this service.

Link: `https://www.youtube.com/watch?v=BrUtQDtYkqE`

QR code:

Cloud Datastore

As an alternative to NoSQL, we also have Cloud Datastore. It is a highly scalable NoSQL database for your mobile and web applications.

Google's BigTable and Megastore technology is used in Cloud Datastore. Let's understand Cloud Datastore in detail.

When to use

Cloud Datastore is ideally used for applications that rely on highly available structured data at scale. Say, you want to store and query data as product catalogs that provide real-time inventory and product details for a retailer.

Cloud Datastore can also be used when storing and querying of user profiles is required. We can use that to deliver a customized experience based on the user's past activities and preferences.

But there is constraint with Cloud Datastore: we cannot use it for effective storage solutions for analytics as it is not a relational database.

Special features

Let's discuss the features that Cloud Datastore has to offer. Cloud Datastore is a highly scalable NoSQL database with high availability and durability. It is also fully managed, which means it automatically handles sharding and replication.

The power of ACID transactions also plays a role when using Cloud Datastore. It provides capabilities as ACID transactions, SQL-like queries, and indexes, at the same time being a schemaless database. We can access Cloud Datastore via JSON API, open source clients, or community-maintained ORMs (Objectify or NDB).

Encryption at rest, atomic transactions, and a balance of strong and eventual consistency are a few other features of GCP.

How to use Cloud Datastore - Video

Below is the video that will explain you how to use this service.

Link: `https://www.youtube.com/watch?v=roIYM10vHGY`

QR code:

Persistent disks

Persistent disks are network storage devices that are durable and have high performance. The disks can be attached to and accessed by the instances. These devices can be used with Google Compute Engine or Google Kubernetes Engine.

Automatic encryption helps us in protecting the disks. We can resize your storage while it is still being used by VMs with no downtime, but you might face some performance issue, though negligible ones.

When to use

We will be using persistent disks when we need reliable and affordable storage with consistent performance characteristics. With standard HDD persistent disks, they are efficient and economical for handling sequential read and write operations. Random IOPS are not optimized on persistent disks.

At the same time, SSDs are used for high rates of random input/output operations per second. These are designed for single-digit millisecond latencies, but often they are not used for archival purposes.

We can use local SSDs that are suitable for temporary storage. SSDs can also be used when we need fast scratch disk or cache, processing space, or low-value data.

Special feature

We will be discussing the different features persistent disk has to offer; they all fall under block storage devices. Here, a block is a record or collection of records. It is a sequence of bytes or bits. It has a a maximum length, called Block Size.

Block storage is usually deployed in a **storage area network** (**SAN**) environment and they are accessible through a **fiber channel** (**FC**) or iSCSI. But for us as user, each block can be controlled as an individual hard drive, which is controlled by a server-based OS. We can format each block individually with the required filesystem, such as NTFS, VMFS (VMware), SMB (Windows), and NFS.

Persistent Disks are located independently from VM instances; that means we can detach or move a persistent disk while still keeping the data.

We have two types of persistent disks, standard HDD and SSD:

- Standard HDD uses magnetic storage to store and retrieve digital information. These are non-volatile and retain data even when powered off.
- SSDs use integrated circuit assemblies as memory to store data persistently. SSDs don't have any moving mechanical components, so they have lower access time and lower latency.

SSDs are also divided into two categories: SSD persistent disk and Local SSD. SSDs act as a cache for most frequently used data. Local SSDs are physically attached to the server running the instance. Lower latency and higher throughput are provided by local SSDs than standard persistent disks or SSD persistent disks. Local SSDs are available through either the SCSI interface or the NVMe interface.

Other features that persistent disks offer are ease of use and best performance with a single filesystem with no partition tables. One should prefer multiple disks over multiple partitions—the same strategy that we apply while working with Windows.

Performance is one more factor here; block storage performance for a given application can be categorized into two distinct IO patterns:

- **Small reads and writes**: recognized by random IOPS per second
- **Large reads and writes**: recognized by throughput

A persistent disk can scale automatically and linearly with size, at the same time providing lower latency than Google Cloud Storage. We can also resize it to provide more space, improved throughput, and IOPS. Cumulative network egress traffic is contributed to each persistent disk write operation.

On the basis of the interface you select, such as SCSI or NVMe, the performance of local SSD varies heavily. For best local SSD performance, combine multiple local SSD devices into a single volume and format local SSD devices individually.

Reliability goes hand in hand with persistent disk. We have built-in redundancy to protect data against equipment failure. Persistent snapshots also ensure data availability. We can create snapshots of persistent disks even if the disks are detached from any of the running instances.

Disk can be encrypted with either system-defined keys or customer-supplied keys. On deletion of the disk, the keys are discarded, making the data irretrievable. You also need to take care of the fact that customer-supplied encryption keys cannot be used with local SSDs, if you are considering so.

We have some obvious limitations with each persistent disk. One is that the maximum storage capacity can be 64 TB only. The number of persistent disks to be attached depends on the number of vCPUs in that instance; the more the vCPUs, the more the disks that can be attached. Like predefined machine types, we can have up to 128 persistent disks per instance. And for customer machine types, we can have up to 16 persistent disks per instance.

Data Persistence in a persistent disk of type local SSDs persists only if you reboot your guest OS, if you configure your instance for live migration, and if the host system experiences a host error, the Compute Engine attempts to preserve the local SSD data only if the underlying drive recovers in 60 minutes.

The data on local SSD doesn't persist in scenarios like these: if we terminate our instance manually, shutting down the guest OS, the instance terminates on host maintenance events. We cannot persist data on a local SSD when the instance is a pre-emptible instance or the local SSD is misconfigured and not reachable.

Now let's know more about standard hard disk drives, solid-state drives, and persistent disks.

Standard hard disk drive

A standard hard disk drive is a non-volatile storage that retains stored data even when powered off. It is a data storage device that uses magnetic storage to store and retrieve the data. Rapidly rotating disks or platters coated with magnetic material are used to perform these operations. Data is accessed in a random-access manner, thus making it slow. Individual blocks can be stored or retrieved in any order and not only sequentially.

Solid-state drives

SSDs store data in electrical charges, which slowly leaks over time if left without power. We cannot use SSDs for archival purposes, as a slow leak of electrical charges causes worn out drives to start losing data typically after 1 or 2 years in storage.

SSDs are storage devices that use integrated circuit assemblies as memory to store data persistently. SSD technology primarily uses electronic interfaces compatible with traditional block input/output hard disk drives. SSDs have no moving mechanical components; therefore, SSDs are typically more resistant to physical shock, run silently, and have quicker access time and lower latency.

Persistent disk

The Compute Engine manages physical disks and data distribution to ensure redundancy and optimize performance. Persistent disks are durable network storage devices that can be accessed by instances like any physical disks in a desktop or server. The data on each persistent disk is distributed across several physical disks.

Persistent disks are available in two-forms:

- Standard hard disk drives
- Solid-state drives

Persistent disks are located independently from the virtual machine. The disks can be detached from the instances and still keep the data. The size of a persistent disk can be resized. The performance of a persistent disk scales automatically with the size of the disk.

How to attache Persistent Store to VM - Video

Below is the video that will explain you how to use this service.

Link: https://www.youtube.com/watch?v=xWx1G85EKjA

QR code:

Summary

And thus, with this, we are done with the chapter. We focused deeply on the eight different and major services in GCP related to ingestion and storing. We focused on and learned about Cloud Dataflow, Cloud Pub/Sub, Cloud Storage, Cloud SQL, Cloud BigTable, Cloud Spanner, Cloud Datastore, and Persistent Disks.

We delved into, and came to understand, the different options in ingestion and storage.

The next chapter is about services related to processing and visualizing. See you there!!

Processing and Visualizing – Close Encounter

In the previous chapter, we learned about various services of GCP in ingestion and storage. In this chapter, we go ahead with processing and visualizing services. Here, we will be discussing all the major services Google Cloud Platform has to offer in processing data and visualizing it.

The list of the topics goes as follows:

- BigQuery
- Cloud Dataproc
- Cloud Datalab
- Google Data Studio
- Compute Engine
- App Engine
- Container Engine
- Cloud Functions

Google BigQuery

Google BigQuery is a framework created by Google that helps to execute SQL-like queries on vast amounts of data at great speeds. Your own dataset can be uploaded to BigQuery, or for sandbox play, some other dataset can be used. The Results can be captured and stored on Google Cloud or can be downloaded as a CSV/Excel file on a local system.

Google BigQuery is a data warehouse framework that resolves problems by enabling super-fast SQL queries, using the execution power of Google's infra services. Also, any data can be updated or monitored based on the business needs. It can even provide others the ability to view or execute some queries on the data. BigQuery can be accessed by using a web User Interface or command-line argument; you can even make calls to the BigQuery REST API using a variety of client libraries such as Java, .NET, or Python. Also there are a variety of third-party tools that you can use to interact with BigQuery for visualizing or loading data.

Storing data in BigQuery

Using BigQuery, we can save multiple types of data, such as structured data. Also, it supports multiple technical solutions, such as compression, replication, encryption, and scaling, as well as performance tuning of data and executing queries at the same time. BigQuery has a feature to store data in the Capacitor columnar data format. BigQuery can also represent the standard database structures: tables, partitions, columns, and rows. To perform any operations on BigQuery, we need to first load the data into BigQuery, and then we can execute queries.

You can load data with the help of Google Cloud Storage that has been stored in any form, be it image, text, or media. With the help of a readable data source, you can load data in BigQuery in batches. Also, using streaming inserts of individual records is also possible.

Bulk inserts can be performed using DML statements. We can also write data to BigQuery with the help of the Google Cloud Dataflow pipeline.

The data can be uploaded or appended, or existing data can be overwritten into a new table, existing table, or partitions. When data gets loaded into BigQuery, a table name can be provided or the partition schema can be defined. Also, for supported data formats, schema auto-detection feature can be useful.

Features of BigQuery

BigQuery comes with many features. We can go for data ingestion in batch mode as well as streaming mode. The pricing of BigQuery is pay-per-query. BigQuery provides you with two execution engines:

- Google Dremel Execution Engine
- Standard SQL

You are free to use the one you want.

It has a serverless service model and an optimized storage engine. The Jupyter network helps to maintain a separation between storage and compute. Cloud IAM is well integrated with BigQuery.

Choosing a data ingestion format

You can load data into BigQuery in a number of different ways using different formats. When the data is uploaded using any tool into BigQuery, it is converted into columnar format for the Capacitor. The Capacitor is a type of storage format used in BigQuery. Depending on the following factors, we can choose the right format.

Schema type of the data

We can receive data in the form of flat file like JSON, CSV, Avro, and Parquet. Avro, Parquet, Cloud Datastore backups, and JSON support data with nested and repeated fields. Nested and repeated data is useful for expressing hierarchical data; JSON, Parquet, and Cloud Datastore reduce data duplication as they support nested data storage while normalizing the data.

External limitations

The data might be sourced from a document store database or from MongoDB; it mostly stores data in JSON format. Also, the data might be imported from a source that only exports in CSV format.

Embedded newlines

BigQuery expects newline-delimited JSON files to contain a single record per line if the data contains embedded newlines in it. BigQuery will upload data faster in JSON or Avro format. While loading data from JSON files, the rows must be of newline delimited in loaded.

Supported data formats

BigQuery supports loading data from the following two data sources in there supporting formats:

- Google Cloud Storage
- Readable data source

We will discuss each of them in the coming sections.

Google Cloud Storage

- Avro
- JSON
- CSV
- Google Cloud Datastore backups

Readable data source

- Avro format
- CSV (this is the default storage format)
- JSON

Once the data is loaded, we can perform the following data operations:

- Analyzing or querying the tables using SQL
- Modifying data using SQL exporting data (DML)
- Copying tables from one source to another

Use case

In the following use case, we will be discussing how BigQuery and PubSub can be used to stream Twitter data to BigQuery. The architecture is as follows for this use case. Let's discuss that in more detail:

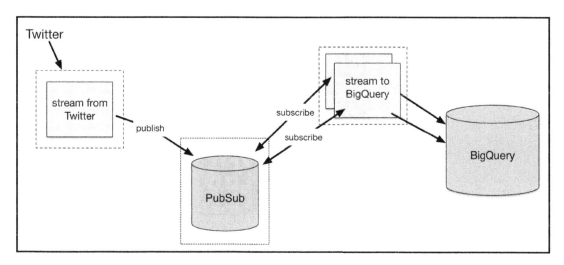

Here, we have the requirement of streaming Twitter data using Cloud PubSub to Cloud BigQuery and performing analytics on top of it. Therefore, we first have to create an application on Twitter. This Twitter application will give us authority to access Twitter tweets.

Then we will create a topic in Cloud PubSub, and also a Google Kubernetes Engine cluster. Now we have to publish Twitter streaming data to Cloud PubSub. And CLoud BigQuery is required to subscribe to this topic to get the data. The moment BigQuery is subscribed to Cloud PubSub, it will start receiving data and then you can run your queries on the top of it.

How to use Google BigQuery - Video

Below is the video to understand how to use the given service.

Link: https://www.youtube.com/watch?v=pj31-RXpduQ

QR code:

Cloud Dataproc

Cloud Dataproc is the service that helps enterprises to have Spark and Hadoop integrated services in just a few minutes. It enables us to use open source data tools for batch processing of data, query operations on data, streaming process of data, and applying machine learning algorithms to data.

Cloud Dataproc's feature of orchestration is useful to create clusters quickly, manage them easily, and save money by turning clusters off when not in use. Cloud Dataproc has a minimum cost based on the actual use of it while processing the data, and it is measured second-wise, which is a very unique model BTW. Cloud Dataproc clusters are included like a lower-cost, pre-emptible instance, which gives powerful clusters with the well monitored mechanism at a minimum cost.

Cloud Dataproc handles creation and management of cluster and job orchestration required in a project, which is unlike the Hadoop framework. It has a powerful set of control and integration operations, which monitor the life cycle management and does other monitoring of the clusters. Cloud Dataproc can be integrated with the YARN application manager to manage and easily access the cluster.

In addition, Cloud Dataproc supports different types of jobs, which includes a job of Spark SQL, a job of MapReduce, or maybe a Hive query, a script written in Pig, and PySpark jobs.

When to use it

Cloud Dataproc is useful when you have your current Data Analytics platform on the Hadoop ecosystem or you want to leverage the open source Hadoop ecosystem. The good thing is that if you are moving from in-house to cloud, you don't have to work on any redevelopment of the code, nor on ETL pipelines.

This is very quick and can be used for temporary jobs as well.

Features of Dataproc

Now we will be discussing the different features that Dataproc has to offer.

Super-fast to build the cluster

Cloud Dataproc can be used in cluster creation, which can now be much faster and can be built in 90 seconds or less. Without using Cloud Dataproc, it can take 5 to 30 minutes (or sometimes weeks) to create Spark and Hadoop integrated clusters or via IaaS providers. This clearly means that it spends less time on waiting for cluster creation, so we can get more hands-on time working with our data.

With this fast cluster building, you can start a cluster when required, process your data, and delete the cluster, thus spending very little for some very huge work.

Low cost

Cloud Dataproc is very cheap—the pricing as low as 1 cent per virtual CPU in the cluster per hour on top of other Cloud Platform resources. Also, you can involve the pre-emptible instances in Cloud Dataproc clusters that may have lower computation prices on an hourly basis; this can reduce the costs to a great extent, effectively leading to huge savings. Cloud Dataproc charges for second-by-second billing and a low 1-minute minimum billing period instead of rounding the usage up to the nearest hour, which is the case with most other cloud vendors.

Easily integrated with other components

Cloud Dataproc also has built-in integration with other Google Cloud Platform services, such as Cloud Storage, BigQuery, and Bigtable. So, along with a Spark or Hadoop cluster, we can set up a complete data platform. For example, you can use Cloud Dataproc to effortlessly get ETL and terabytes of raw log data directly into BigQuery for business reporting.

Another use case of Cloud Storage object storage is storing data that needs to be processed in Dataproc instead of using Hadoop Distributed File System.

Available versions and supported components of Cloud DataProc

The latest version of Cloud Dataproc is 1.2, which was released in July 2017 and is now the default version for new cluster setup. This latest version supports the following components:

- Apache Spark 2.2.0
- Apache Hadoop 2.8.2
- Apache Pig 0.16.0
- Apache Hive 2.1.1
- Google Cloud Storage Connector 1.6.3 – Hadoop 2
- BigQuery connector 0.10.4 – Hadoop 2

These versions keep on getting updated by GCP's Cloud Dataproc team.

Accessibility of Google Cloud Dataproc

We can access Cloud Dataproc using the following options:

- Via Cloud SDK
- Using the REST API
- Through the Cloud Dataproc

So, accessing Cloud Dataproc is not a challenge in any way.

Placement of Dataproc

The following is a typical placement of Dataproc. Let's talk more about it:

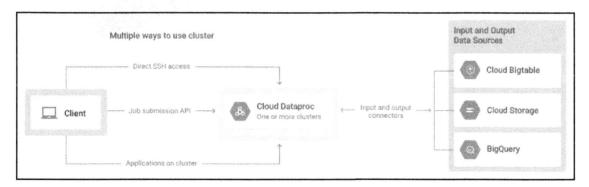

In the preceding diagram, you can see that we have **Cloud Dataproc** connected with **Cloud Bigtable**, **Cloud Storage**, and **BigQuery**. **Client** means the users who are accessing **Cloud Dataproc**. Thus, all of the data that is being processed can be stored or further analyzed on other GCP services. This makes it very handy when it comes to working on different and more complex use cases on the cloud.

Dataflow versus Dataproc

The following should be your flowchart when choosing Dataproc or Dataflow:

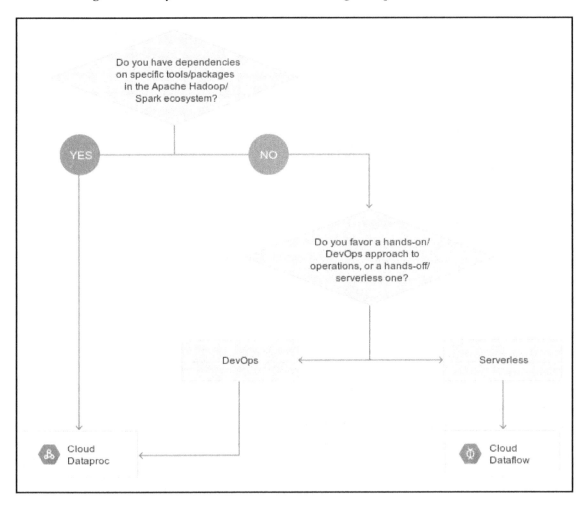

A table-based comparison of Dataproc versus Dataflow:

Workload	Cloud Dataproc	Cloud Dataflow
Stream processing (ETL)	No	Yes
Batch processing (ETL)	Yes	Yes

Workload	Cloud Dataproc	Cloud Dataflow
Iterative processing and notebooks	Yes	No
Machine learning with Spark ML	Yes	No
Preprocessing for machine learning	NO	Yes (with Cloud ML Engine)

Pricing

The pricing totally depends on the size and data used in Cloud Dataproc clusters; it can also be measured as per the execution time and duration. The size of the cluster depends on the aggregate number of virtual CPUs (vCPUs) across the entire cluster that is, worker and master nodes. The duration of a cluster is the length of time between cluster creation and cluster deletion measured in minutes.

You can visit https://cloud.google.com/dataproc/pricing for more information about pricing.

How to use Cloud Dataproc - Video

Below is the video to understand how to use the given service.

Link: https://www.youtube.com/watch?v=dZL1VAn2ITI

QR code:

Google Cloud Datalab

Google recently has launched a tool for data analysis and performing data operations using cloud, named Cloud Datalab. It is a perfect integration of the IPython Jupyter notebook system with Google's BigQuery data warehouse, along with many more nice features of Datalab. It also integrates standard Python libraries, such as graphics and scikit-learn, and Google's own machine learning toolkit TensorFlow.

Cloud Datalab is executed on a VM instance, which is packaged as a container. We can establish a connection from our browser to the Cloud Datalab container. Thus we can open existing Cloud Datalab notebooks and create the new notebooks. Notebooks are used by Cloud Datalab to store and write the code and not the plaintext files. Notebooks integrate the code together and the documentation is written as markdown, along with the results of code execution, whether it could be a text, image, or HTML/JavaScript, we can use Notebooks very similar to we writing a code in editor similar to IDE. It helps to execute the code step by step in an interactive and iterative manner effectively, at the same time storing the results alongside the code.

You can store Cloud Datalab notebooks on the Google Cloud Source Repository. As well, you can clone the GIT repository code onto a persistent disk attached to the VM. And it will create the workspace used in the project. In this workspace, addition of files, removal of file, and the modify files type of operation can be performed. Sharing this work with other users is possible by making a commit to a GIT client into the GIT and pushing it from local workspace to the repository. At a regular intervals, we can also save the code, or at any time; Notebooks are auto saved to the persistent disk in the cluster.

After opening the notebook, a backend kernel process is launched. It is launched to manage the variables that are defined early during the session and executes your notebook code. The executed code might be using the BigQuery and Google Machine Learning Engine; it will automatically enable the service account available in the VM. The VM is a shared resource used for running Cloud Datalab. Using an individual's personal cloud credentials to access data is strongly discouraged.

The service uses Jupyter notebooks/IPython, a format that allows you to create documents with live code and visualizations. Jupyter is one of the most popular tools in the data science world, and a number of ecosystems have grown around it, which should make getting started with this new Google tool easier too.

Features of Cloud DataLab

Now we will discuss the different features of Cloud Datalab.

Multi-language support

Cloud Datalab has support for multiple languages. This includes Python, SQL, and JavaScript to write the code for building pipelines and storing data.

Integration with multiple Google services

With Cloud BigQuery, Cloud Machine Learning Engine, Cloud Storage, and Stackdriver monitoring, Cloud Datalab simplifies data processing. Other aspects, such as authentication, cloud computation, and source control are taken care of as well.

Interactive data visualization

We can use Google Data Studio for easy visualizations; it is very well integrated with Cloud Datalab.

Machine learning

Along with scikit-learn, it supports TensorFlow-based deep ML models. It also scales training and prediction via specialized libraries for Cloud Machine Learning Engine.

Use case

Cloud Datalab is a data analysis and machine learning approach designed for Google Cloud Platform. It can be used to explore data, analyze it, transform it from one form to another, visualize it interactively, and also create machine learning models out of the data. Along with all this support, it contains a set of commonly used open source Python libraries used for data analysis, visualization, and machine learning. There are also libraries for accessing Google Cloud Platform services, such as Google BigQuery, Google Machine Learning Engine, Dataflow, and Cloud Storage.

How to use Google Cloud Datalab - Video

Below is the video to understand how to use the given service.

Link: https://www.youtube.com/watch?v=eQjMg851uPY

QR code:

Google Data Studio

In the GCP ecosystem, along with data crunching, we also require data representation and telling stories by graphical representation. Therefore, to fulfill this requirement, we have Google Data Studio. It is a very popular visualization tool used to create a graph and chart so as to represent the data to the business owner. Using Data Studio, we combine the data from a variety of sources for reporting and analysis and share dashboards. We can also filter data at the report, page, or chart level. And the best part is that Data Sudio is absolutely free to use, while comparing Data Studio with Tableau or Power Bl.

Features of Data Studio

The following are the features of Google Data Studio.

Data connections

One of the major challenges of data reporting tools has always been the ability to access and bring all the data together. Google Data Studio easily manages this by simplifying the process—by providing the prebuilt data connectors you need.

We have connectors to connect to Google BigQuery, Data Connectors, DoubleClick, Google AdWords, MySQL, and many others.

Data visualization and customization

By building amazing visualization and customization solutions, Data Studio helps us to engage and create a beautiful data story that can help lure our customers. As we already know, reports and dashboards are the standard media for communicating analyzed data to business people, as most business decisions are often taken by reading graphs and charts. Whether you are editing an existing report or starting from scratch to create the report, that data studio helps you in a very easy, clearly, and most importantly is in the more presented and visualize manner.

Usability

A super easy drag-and-drop type of facility by Google Data Studio helps to build reports on the dashboard. Due to the ease of use of its functions and accessibility, most frontend developers will like Data Studio.

Data transformation

The data often needs to be transformed into more complete and meaningful information, as functions and creating charts and graphs are easy in data studio. We can create powerful building blocks for charts and graphs using Data Studio to create our data's dimensions and metrics.

Sharing and collaboration

This is one more amazing feature. We can work with our team when creating the same dashboard and suggest the color that we want it to use; after all, color is an important aspect of presentation.

Report templates

Google Data Studio offers you a library of report templates to choose from. They will help you to be up and running in minutes. Simply connect your data sources and customize the design and style to match your needs.

Report customization

If you are not very comfortable with report templates, then you can also customize your reports. Data Studio lets you update or create every aspect of reports and dashboards for business purposes such that you can create it all your way. From changing the background texture to filling the gaps to inserting the line along with text colors and adding icons or logos, you can choose from an array of fonts, line styles, and object properties to build. Dynamic control is another feature that allows viewers to interact and explore data in real time.

The flow of Data Studio

To understand the complete flow of Data Studio, we can have a look at the following image. Data Studio will have four major parts:

- Connect
- Analyze
- Visualize
- Share

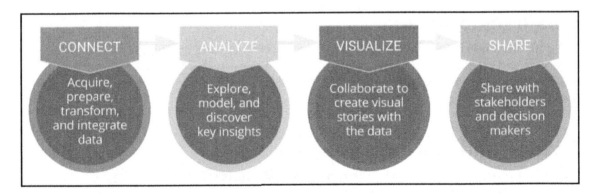

The first and most important task for us is to connect Data Studio with the data source; without data, we cannot do anything. The next step is to analyze; we can do that by using multiple services that GCP has to offer. Once we are done with exploring, modeling, and finding some key insights, it's time for representation. Representation plays a key role in hitting the right chord. And then, we all are good with sharing our charts and graphs.

How to use Google Data Studio - Video

Below is the video to understand how to use the given service.

Link: `https://www.youtube.com/watch?v=RUklrAMSsyY`

QR code:

Google Compute Engine

Google Compute Engine is the service in GCP that helps us in provisioning virtual machines as per our requirements; we have the option to customize it and run it as long as we want, while getting amazing discounts for running it for a longer duration. While creating a VM, you have the option of creating a Linux instance; at the same time, you can create a Windows instance as well.

Compute Engine offers scale, performance, and value, allowing you to easily launch large compute clusters on Google's infrastructure. Plus you don't have any upfront investments, and you can run thousands of virtual CPUs on a system that has been designed to be fast and offer strong consistency of performance.

You can create your own VPC and provision a custom VM. Due to this characteristic of Compute Engine, users can host the same logic in the cloud as is currently hosted on the physical infrastructure and on virtual machines provided by Google.

We can create virtual machine instances in the corresponding regions, shown as follows:

North America				South America
northamerica-northeast1	**us-west1**	**us-central1**		**southamerica-east1**
'northamerica-northeast1-a'	'us-west1-a'	'us-central1-a'		'southamerica-east1-a'
'northamerica-northeast1-b'	'us-west1-b'	'us-central1-b'		'southamerica-east1-b'
'northamerica-northeast1-c'	'us-west1-c'	'us-central1-c'		'southamerica-east1-c'
		'us-central1-f'		
	us-east1	**us-east4**		
	'us-east1-b'	'us-east4-a'		
	'us-east1-c'	'us-east4-b'		
	'us-east1-d'	'us-east4-c'		

Europe		Asia		Australia
europe-west1	**europe-west2**	**asia-northeast1**	**asia-east1**	**australia-southeast1**
'europe-west1-b'	'europe-west2-a'	'asia-northeast1-a'	'asia-east1-a'	'australia-southeast1-a'
'europe-west1-c'	'europe-west2-b'	'asia-northeast1-b'	'asia-east1-b'	'australia-southeast1-b'
'europe-west1-d'	'europe-west2-c'	'asia-northeast1-c'	'asia-east1-c'	'australia-southeast1-c'
europe-west3	**europe-west4**	**asia-southeast1**	**asia-south1**	
'europe-west3-a'	'europe-west4-a'	'asia-southeast1-a'	'asia-south1-a'	
'europe-west3-b'	'europe-west4-b'	'asia-southeast1-b'	'asia-south1-b'	
'europe-west3-c'	'europe-west4-c'		'asia-south1-c'	

You can visit this link to get an idea of the regions in more detail: `https://cloud.google.com/compute/docs/regions-zones`.

Features

Google Computer Engine has many features. For instance, it has really start fast-booting (it boots up very fast). You have complete freedom to customize your virtual machine instances and they are consistently high-performance. GCP has offered you a variety of Linux and Windows OS images to choose from for your instance.

You also have multiple block storage options, like SSD and HDD. You can opt for the one that best suits the price, performance, and durability requirements of your application.

And then we safely broadcast the virtual machine instances on the Web using an easily configurable firewall. We can easily monitor the instances and infrastructure via a simple REST API, robust command-line tool, or the simple yet powerful web-based Google Cloud Platform Console.

Advantages of Compute Engine

The following are the major advantages of Compute Engine.

Batch processing

We can use the highly cost-effective Compute Engine to run large compute and batch jobs using pre-emptible VMs. One of the main advantage of pre-emptible instances is its pricing. It does not vary and is approximately fixed. And no contracts or predefined reservations! That makes it easier for batch processing. For this, you have to simply check a box when you create the VM and turn it off when the work is done.

Predefined machine types

We studied in the preceding topic about pre-emptible instances; let's know exactly what they are. Pre-emptible instances are Compute Engine instances consisting of predefined virtual machine instance configurations for every need, from micro instances to as much as 96 vCPUs or 624GB of memory. They come in variations of standard, high-memory, and high-CPU configurations.

Persistent disks

The maximum storage we can associate with a VM is approx 64TB in size; that can be used with VMs as persistent disks. Also, the persistent disks can be created in any format, such as HDD or SSD. If one of the virtual instances is terminated or damaged, we can recover the data in the persistent disk and attach persistent disk to another virtual machine instance. Similarly, we can also take a copy or create an image of the persistent disk and create new persistent disks from that snapshot to create a new VM.

Linux and Windows support

Supported Linux OSes are Debian, CentOS, SUSE, Ubuntu, Red Hat, and FreeBSD. While for Windows, it is Windows Server 2008 R2, 2012 R2, and 2016. You can also use a shared image from the Cloud Platform community.

Per-second billing

Google bills in second-level increments. You pay only for the compute time that you use.

Types of Compute Engine

We have three different types of Compute Engine:

- Quickstart VM
- Custom VM
- Preemptible VM

Let's discuss them one by one.

Quickstart VM

Quickstart VM is provided by GCP Compute Engine by default in its list of VMs. While initiating the VM, you will be given a drop-down list by GCP and you can choose any one of them as per your requirements.

Custom VM

Custom VMs are something that GCP Compute Engine does not have in its list of VMs, but we can create one of our own with respect to the amount of CPUs and memory we need as per our application requirements.

You can create them in a CLI, as follows:

```
//CREATE INSTANCE WITH 4 vCPUs and 5 GB MEMORY
gcloud compute instances create my-vm --custom-cpu 4 --custom-memory 5
```

Preemptible VM

Preemptible VMs are the ones we use for a shorter time span, ranging from a few minutes to 24 hours. They are typically used for fault-tolerant applications, such as media transcoding or building a Hadoop cluster.

You can start a preemptible VM using the following command in the CLI:

```
// ENABLE PREEMPTIBLE OPTION
gcloud compute instances create my-vm --zone us-central1-b --preemptible
```

Use case

We can create high-performance computing clusters by utilizing Google Compute Engine VMs and Google Cloud Storage. The customer can run all the jobs using running HPC workloads of the application on Google's Cloud.

In the following diagram, you can see how we can have multiple Compute Engines (Compute Nodes) attached to a Compute Engine (HPC Head). At the same time, we are using multiple Compute Engines as a filesystem:

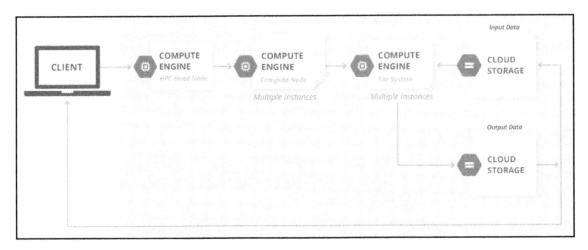

The compute portion of the cluster contains a Head Node running as orchestration software on a Google Compute Engine instance. The compute nodes and the related worker nodes are executing their task on Google Compute Engine virtual machine instances. We can select the instance type to match the workload. We can choose from Standard, High-Memory, or High-CPU instances in the core size range of 1, 2, 4, 8, or 16. You can also delete or add instances depending on the resources needed. Moreover, you can create a cluster of various commercial packages or open source software components as per your own choice.

Want to create a filesystem type of model to use in the cluster? A Compute Engine instance can serve that purpose as well! The two most common options are NFS and Cluster. NFS and Clusters are now the optional components as there is direct access to Compute Nodes using Google Cloud Storage. Thus, we can store data directly on Cloud Storage as well.

Google Cloud Storage provides backend storage for the cluster, providing a storage option with high availability and durability and making it an excellent choice for HPC work. Google Cloud SQL is also available for structured input or output data. The source data can be uploaded into Cloud Storage also; that can be done by running a job. The resulting data can be downloaded on the client or left in the cloud for storage or further processing.

How to use Google Compute Engine - Video

Below is the video to understand how to use the given service.

Link: `https://www.youtube.com/watch?v=-kzY5VymiMI`

QR code:

Google App Engine

Google App Engine was developed as a PaaS for apps and to provide a mobile backend, with the feature of scalability in mind. It is used in cloud computing platforms for developing and hosting web applications. We have two different environments to host a web application: Flexible Environment and Standard Environment. Depending on the features and advantages available for both, any of them can be adopted.

Characteristics of flexible and standard environments

The following are the features of a flexible environment and a standard environment:

Feature	Flexible environment	Standard environment
Maximum request timeout	60 minutes	60 seconds
Instance startup time	Minutes	Seconds
Background threads	Yes	Yes, but with restrictions

Background processes	Yes	No
Scaling	Manual, automatic	Manual, basic
Writing to local disk	Yes	No
Modifying the runtime	Yes	No
Network access	Yes	Only via App Engine services
Supports installing third-party binaries	Yes	No
Pricing	Based on vCPU and memory	Based on instance hours

The application can be run in App Engine using a flexible environment or standard environment. Apart from that, it is possible to implement both the environments in a single application, just to leverage the advantages of each individual environment.

Google AppEngine architecture

App Engine provides a robust environment to create web applications. Supported languages are Java, Python, and PI-IP. Development and deployment of the application to the cloud is well supported by App Engine. App Engine can easily handle updates to new application features and manage the data traffic. AppEngine is divided into two major types - Standard and Flexible.

Standard environment has a integration of Memcache and Task Queue services in the standard App Engine environment. Memcache is an in-memory cache that is shared across App Engine instances. This is used to achieve extremely-high-speed access to get information cached by the web server (for example, authentication or account information).

Whereas Task Queues helps to provide a mechanism to reduce the load of longer-running tasks to backend servers; it also frees the frontend servers so as to service new user requests. Finally, App Engine contains the built-in load balancer, which is by default provided by Google Load Balancer. Load balancers provide transparent Layer 3 and Layer 7 load balancing to applications.

Features

Let's discuss the features of App Engine.

Multiple language support

Language support is very good in App Engine. Be it Node.js, Java, Ruby, C#, Go, Python, or PHP, the user can code in the language of their choice.

Application versioning

App Engine has an easy-to-use and good interface for hosting different versions of your app. Not only that, but you can also easily create development, test, staging, and production environments in a few clicks.

Fully managed

Fully managed is a very beautiful phrase in GCP, and you can associate it with App Engine!

Application security

We can have predefined access rules to safeguard the application. This can be done by the App Engine firewall, and managed SSUTLS certificates are leveraged by default on your custom domain at no additional cost.

Traffic splitting

Route incoming requests to different app versions and do incremental feature rollouts. An amazing feature to have!

Use case

The following is a generic use case we can have when including App Engine and Firebase. Let's learn a bit about them:

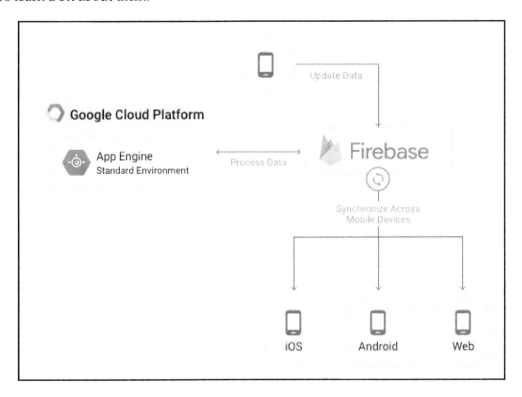

In the preceding diagram, you can see that we have Firebase. Firebase is a database-as-a-service service in GCP. It provides a backend database to the application. As we can see in the preceding diagram, we have updated the data coming to Firebase from some unknown source; let's assume it's another app. Firebase is receiving the data from that app and processing it with the help of Standard App Engine. Once the data is processed, we transmit the processed data to iOS, Android, and Web.

In this manner, App Engine can be used where we are least worried about our infrastructure.

How to use Google App Engine - Video

Below is the video to understand how to use the given service.

Link: `https://www.youtube.com/watch?v=Euto64w21uU`

QR code:

Google Container Engine

Google Container Engine is also known as Google Kubernetes Engine or GKE. GKE is a management and orchestration system for Docker containers, the container clusters run within Google's public cloud services, on Google Compute Engine.

Kubernetes is Google's open source container management system. Users can use the *gcloud* command-line interface or the Google Cloud Platform Console to interact with Google Kubernetes Engine.

The typical users of Google Kubernetes Engine are software developers. They create, deploy, and test new enterprise applications from time to time. To better meet the scalability and performance demands of enterprise applications, administrators also use containers. Kubernetes runs on a cluster of Google Compute Engine; we call it Google Kubernetes Engine, which has Kubernetes running on it.

Docker containers are managed by a master node as a cluster master. To perform tasks such as servicing API requests and scheduling containers, it also runs a Kubernetes API server to interact with the cluster. A cluster can also include one or more nodes beyond the master node. Each of them runs a Docker runtime and kubelet agent. These components are needed to manage Docker containers.

Google Kubernetes Engine users organize one or more containers into pods to represent logical groups of related containers. Say, these groups could include log filesystem containers, checkpoint system containers, and data compression containers. Similarly, network proxies, bridges, and adapters can be organized into the same pod. As a best practice, identical containers are not organized into the same pod.

Container cluster architecture

A container cluster consists of at least one cluster master and many worker machines called nodes. These master and node machines have the responsibility to run the Kubernetes cluster orchestration system.

For Kubernetes Engine, a container cluster can be considered the foundation. On top of a cluster runs the containerized applications.

Cluster master

The Kubernetes plane processes is controlled by the cluster master. The Kubernetes API scheduler, core resource controllers, and server are controlled by the cluster master. Kubernetes Engine manages the master's lifecycle by creating or deleting a cluster. Kubernetes Engine often performs automatically or manually upgrades to the Kubernetes version running on the cluster master. This process depends on whether you are requesting to prefer an upgrade earlier than the automatic schedule.

Cluster master and the Kubernetes API

The unified endpoint for your cluster is the master. Kubernetes API calls are used to perform all interactions with the cluster. While the Kubernetes API Server runs on the master, it handles all those requests. We can make direct Kubernetes API calls, which can be made via HTTP/gRPC. The API calls can be made indirectly as well, by running commands from the Kubernetes CLI (kubectl) or by interacting with the UI in the GCP Console.

Master and node interaction

The Cluster master decides what runs on all of the clusters's nodes. This includes upgrades, managing the workloads life cycle, scaling, and scheduling workloads. Network and storage resources for those workloads are also managed by the master.

Kubernetes APIs are used by the master and nodes for communication.

Nodes

A container cluster typically has one or more nodes. When it comes to clusters, it is often the case in most cluster-based frameworks that they have master-slave architecture. These are the worker machines that run your containerized applications and other workloads. When you create a cluster, Compute Engine VM instances are the individual machines that Kubernetes Engine creates on your behalf.

Each node's self-reported update status is sent to the master. Opting for some manual control over the node life cycle is one option, or you can let Kubernetes Engine perform automatic repairs and automatic upgrades on your cluster's nodes—you have that freedom.

The Docker runtime and the Kubernetes node agent (kubelet) are part of node. The services necessary to support the Docker containers that make up your cluster's workloads run on nodes. Communication is done by the agent with the master and the responsibility of starting and running Docker containers is scheduled on that node.

Node machine type

Each node is of a standard Compute Engine machine type. By default, we get an instance of 3.75GB of memory and one virtual CPU. We also have the option to choose a different instance type for the cluster.

How to use Google Container Engine - Video

Below is the video to understand how to use the given service.

Link: `https://www.youtube.com/watch?v=Gi-JwQsRbQs`

QR code:

Google Cloud Functions

Google Cloud Functions is a service where you only submit your code and the responsibility of the infrastructure is completely Google Cloud Platform's. Thus, Google cloud functions in short provide an environment to support in building an application and connecting with cloud services.

We can use Cloud Functions to write very basic single-purpose functions. These functions are attached to events emitted from our services and cloud infrastructure. We are not required to make any provision of any infrastructure or worry about taking care of any infrastructure. Automatic triggering of cloud functions will take place in the case of an event being programmed. Cloud Functions and its applications will take care of infrastructure management.

Cloud functions can be developed in multiple languages in multiple environments on Google Cloud Platform.

Connecting and extending cloud services

We can have a connective layer of logic that lets us write code to connect and extend cloud services by using Cloud Functions. Examples are listening and responding to a file upload to Cloud Storage, a message incoming on a Cloud PubSub topic, or an update made in a log.

Cloud Functions increases existing cloud services by allowing you to address an increasing number of use cases with subjective programming logic. A Google Service Account credential is already held by Cloud Functions to access services, thus making Cloud Functions work flawlessly with the majority of Google Cloud Platform services, such as App Engine, Cloud Storage, and many others.

Functions are serverless

As we know by now, Cloud Functions eliminate the work of managing and maintaining servers, configuring software, updating frameworks, and patching operating systems. Google manages the software and infrastructure parts, making code your only concern. Moreover, provisioning of resources happens automatically in response to events (and we know what events are). This means that a function can scale from a few invocations a day to many millions of invocations without any work from you.

Simple and single-purpose functions can be written using Cloud Functions that are attached to events emitted from cloud services. The execution of Cloud Functions starts when an event is being fired. The code is executed in a fully managed environment and can effectively connect or extend services in Google's cloud. We are not required to provision any infrastructure or worry about managing infrastructure. The best part of using Cloud Functions is that a function can scale from a few triggers a day to many millions of triggers in just a matter of time. That too without any work from you, and you pay only while your function is executing!

Use cases

The following are the use cases that Cloud Functions supports.

IoT

Imagine we have millions of IoT devices streaming data into Cloud PubSub. These events can be taken as triggers for launching Cloud Functions to process, transform, and store data. We will be doing this in a completely serverless manner.

Data processing ETL

This is for listening and responding to Cloud Storage events - the events can be a change in file, creation of new file, updating an existing file, or file being deleted. Using the aforementioned triggers, you can use Cloud Functions to process images, perform video transcoding, validate and transform data, and invoke any service.

Mobile backend

Firebase is Google's mobile platform for application developers. You have the provision of writing your mobile backend in Cloud Functions. And we can have events from Firebase analytics, real-time databases, authentication, and storage on the basis of triggers.

How to use Google Cloud Functions - Video

Below is the video to understand how to use the given service.

Link: https://www.youtube.com/watch?v=_2Re44Z7eFM

QR code:

Summary

Thus, with this, we've understood all the major services in processing and visualizing. We understood numerous services such as BigQuery, Cloud Dataproc, Cloud Dataflow (with the differences between them), Data Studio, Compute Engine, App Engine (and its types), Container Engine (aka Kubernetes), and Cloud Functions.

The next chapter is about machine learning, deep learning, and the associated services in GCP.

6

Machine Learning, Deep Learning, and AI on GCP

In this chapter, we are going to talk predominantly on artificial intelligence and machine learning. In the beginning of the chapter, we will understand what artificial intelligence is, and then we will understand what machine learning is.

After that, we will study all the different services that Google has to offer in its cloud platform.

We will cover the following topics in this chapter:

- Artificial Intelligence
- Machine Learning
- Google Cloud Platform
- Google Cloud Machine Learning Engine
- Cloud Natural Language API
- TensorFlow
- Cloud Speech API
- Cloud Translation API
- Cloud Vision API
- Cloud Video Intelligence
- Dialogflow
- AutoML

Artificial intelligence

Artificial intelligence (**AI**) is part of computer science since 1950s. AI is broader way of building smart devices or computer machines that are able to work intelligently. It's used to create intelligent devices or machines working like humans. The scope of AI is nowadays distributed across the fields of electronics, electrical, mechanical, chemical, physics, and many more domains. The activities that are performed by a computer using AI are complex problem solving, learning, planning, speech recognition, reasoning, perception, the ability to move the devices and manipulate objects, knowledge engineering, machine learning, social intelligence, and robotics.

There are quite a few approaches to solving problems using AI, and these approaches are different sets of concepts or patterns. There is no proper theory or steps or unique method to solve a problem. AI is broadly categorized into three approaches:

- **Computational psychology**: Deals with human like behavior
- **Computational philosophy**: Represents to develop a dynamic and adaptive methodology
- **Computational science**: This is used to build computational devices or machines

These approaches are developed by cybernetics, brain simulation, symbolic, cognitive simulation, statistical, and some integrated approaches.

AI has many tools to solve many problems in computational science. Tools such as search and optimization, logic, probabilistic methods for uncertain reasoning, classifiers, statistical learning methods, artificial neural networks, deep learning, and many more are popular.

AI has found a wide variety of applications in:

- Automobiles
- Healthcare
- Finance and economics
- Video games
- Data mining
- Robot soccer
- Conversational behavior
- Sentiment analysis

Machine learning

Machine learning (ML) is a part of an artificial intelligence developed for the technological development of human knowledge. ML provisions devices to dynamically handle any situation through analysis, self-training, observation, and experience, which makes continuous improvement of decisions in subsequent scenarios. ML is ambiguous with data mining in databases for knowledge engineering. It is focused on predictions based on known facts learned from training data, while data mining focuses on the discovery of unknown facts. Data mining uses many ML methods, whereas ML uses unsupervised learning to improve the user's accuracy. Machine learning and statistics are very closely tied domains.

In computational learning theory, a computation is considered feasible if it can be done in polynomial time. Some classes of functions can be learned in polynomial time and others cannot. The approaches of ML are decision tree learning, association rule learning, artificial neural networks, deep learning (a subpart of ANN), support vector machines, clustering, Bayesian networks, reinforcement learning, genetic algorithms, rule-based machine learning, explanation-based learning, mistake correction, case recording, and many other algorithms.

Applications of machine learning include:

- Syntactic pattern recognition
- Natural language processing
- Search engines
- Computer vision
- Machine perception

Google Cloud Platform

Google Cloud AI provides ML services through its well-defined APIs. These services are very fast, easily scalable, and easy to use in practice. The users can use Neural-network-based machine learning algorithms for better performance of their applications.

The GCP provides various types of applications built on an AI platform and is used in many of Google's products. The user's application customization of ML on neural networks can be done by using AutoML. Optimization of ML is allowed through GCP AI TensorFlow workload APIs. Data storage and retrieval are also made easy through Cloud Storage and Cloud Dataflow services. Users can share their thoughts or experiences and make conversations across all domains and devices. Analytical tools are also provided separately for images, videos, audio or speech, text, and other miscellaneous applications.

In this chapter, the authors have tried to explain the GCP AI platform and explore knowledge on the following APIs with use cases:

- Google Cloud machine learning engine
- Cloud natural language API
- TensorFlow
- Speech API
- Translation API
- Vision API
- Video intelligence API

Google Cloud Machine Learning Engine

This is an API that creates a model in machine learning, and can work on any size and any type of data. A major use of this ML is to train a model and predict from it. The ML engine can use any model to perform large-scale analysis on a cluster for managing online and batch programming. It can support a few thousand users and performs on terabytes of data. This service can easily be combined with other services such as Dataflow, Storage, BigQuery, and so on provided by GCP. The ML Engine lets users build models using DataLab and can also build portable models that work on various devices.

The purpose of Cloud ML Engine is to train a new ML model at scale using the TensorFlow application, and the model is hosted to get predictions on a new set of data.

The ML Engine Workflow can be formatted into the following steps:

1. Evaluating the problem
2. Data exploration and preparation
3. Model development and training
4. Model testing and deployment
5. Operational development and management

The engine makes use of the following components for its functioning:

- REST API
- Google Cloud Client Library
- JSON API
- Python
- Cloud DataLab

Pricing

The Cloud ML Engine charges for training models to get predictions but is free for managing resources on the cloud:

- Training:
    - Predefined Scales per hour:
        - Basic $0.28
        - Standard $2.90
    - Machine per hour:
        - Standard $0.28
        - Large $0.70
- Batch processing: $0.92 per node per hour
- Online Prediction: $0.3 per node per hour

The applications of the ML Engine include:

- To train any model at scale and host these models to generate predictions
- Cloud ML Engine uses the IAM service to manage access to resources
- Additionally, it supports cloud audit log, which is used to generate logs for API operations

Cloud Natural Language API

The **natural language API (NL API)** supports various methods to perform analysis and gist generation on text. This API has several methods, such as the following:

- **Sentiment analysis**: Emotional text is recognized and measured in numerical values

- **Entity analysis**: This highlights popular persons, restaurants, landmarks and so on, measured from highest to lowest in their order of occurrence
- **Syntactic analysis**: The structure of sentences or grammar can be tested, and the response is in the form of sentences and tokens
- **Content classification**: Analyzes and categories of text content

Each of these methods has its own APIs to perform several operations on the language. The result of the request can be either in plain text or in HTML format. Here it is also possible to perform all kinds of operation on a single instance on any language.

The architecture of the NLP API is illustrated in the following figure:

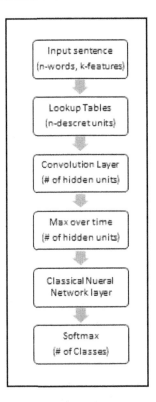

As you can see from the preceding figure, given an input sentence, the API outputs class probabilities for one chosen word. In other words, the purpose of NLP is, making explicit models of human excellence.

The setup makes use of the following components to function:

- REST API
- Google cloud client library
- JSON API
- Cloud endpoints
- Compute engine

Thanks to its wonderful and unique features, the model has found a wide variety of applications, such as:

- Recommender systems
- Predictions
- Expert systems
- Information extraction
- Change work
- Education
- Training
- Sales
- Leadership
- Marketing
- Therapy

 The NL API is free of charge up to 5000 units per month, and beyond this limit, it may charge $1 to $2.

Use Cases

In this section, we will learn the techniques of implementing three different use case:

- Using the goodbooks dataset from github and perform sentiment analysis to find fiction books
- Using GCP services list and classify text based on categories
- State Choice Management (management or controlling of state is a flawed proposition)

We will discuss each of these cases in the coming topics.

Using the goodbooks data set from GitHub

The cloud natural language API can be implemented to perform sentiment analysis function in order to search fiction books from a set of books. The steps to perform the same are as follows:

1. Input the text (the dataset is `books`; it is available at `https://github.com/zygmuntz/goodbooks-10k`)
2. Extract the syntax
3. Sentiment analysis API
4. Generate fiction (positive) or non-fiction books (negative) results
5. Calculate the overall sentiment by adding positive and negative results, is prediction

Using GCP services list and classify text based on categories

Similarly, we can also make use of the API to classify text according to different categories. The steps to implement this technique are as follows:

1. Input the text (in `.csv` format)
2. Query the text based on category
3. Test-split the labels based on category
4. Test the similarity including empty categories
5. Classify the text

State choice management

We can also use the API to control and detect behaviors, using the following steps:

1. Input the current behavioral state
2. Query of chain of excellence with breathing
3. Test with physiology
4. Test with a state change in behavior
5. Know the new state behavioral performance

How to use Natural Language API - Video

Below is the link to the video which you can use to see how this given service is used.

Link: https://www.youtube.com/watch?v=jtRnaxy4vGA

QR code:

TensorFlow

TensorFlow is an open source software library for numerical computation using data flow graphs. Deep learning in the cloud platform is a new type of service facilitated by all Cloud platforms nowadays. This service can use TensorFlow in Google Cloud Platform, which enables users to develop a quick and easy way of application design, development and deployment. TensorFlow for deep learning research and development applications is used in many domains such as natural language processing, speech recognition and translation, and computer vision and so on. TensorFlow is also used to recommend the user to do quick decision making.

The architecture of the TensorFlow model is as follows:

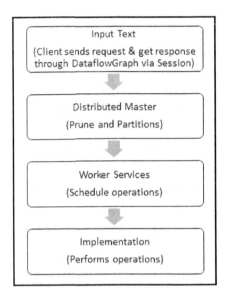

The following components are used in the TensorFlow model:

- Cloud TensorFlow
- Cloud Pub/Sub
- Cloud Dataflow
- Cloud Bigtable
- Cloud BigQuery
- Google Data Studio
- Apigee API Platform
- Cloud Endpoints

The applications of this model include:

- Automotive
- Statistics
- Sentiment analysis in CRM
- Security
- Flaw detection
- Recommendation systems

TensorFlow is an open source machine learning framework for everyone; therefore, no cost!

The advantages of using TensorFlow:

- It has an intuitive construct because, as the name suggests, it has a *flow of tensors*. You can easily visualize each and every part of the graph.
- Easily train on the CPU/GPU for distributed computing.
- Platform flexibility. You can run the models wherever you want, whether it is on mobile, server, or PC.

The limitations of TensorFlow:

- Even though TensorFlow is powerful, it's still a low-level library. For example, it can be considered as a machine-level language; it needs modularity and a high-level interface through the frameworks, such as keras.
- It's still in development, so much more awesomeness to come.
- It depends on your hardware specs; the more the merrier.
- It's still not an API for many languages.
- There are many things yet to be included in TensorFlow, such as OpenCL support.

Use case—text summarization

Summarization is a process to extract parts of the document that are deemed interesting by some metric such as *tf-idf* and join them to form a summary. Algorithms of this flavor are called **extractive summarization**. Another approach is to simply summarize as humans do, which is not to impose the extractive constraint and allow for rephrasing. This is called **abstractive summarization**. The following are the types of text summarization:

- Input text document
- Tokenization
- Stemming
- Building a statistical model on TensorFlow
- Informative word selection and clustering
- Summary generation

Cloud Speech API

A powerful API from GCP! This enables the user to convert speech to text by using a neural network model. This API is used to recognize over 100 languages throughout the world. It can also supports filter of unwanted noise/ content from a text, under various types of environments. It supports for context-awareness recognition, works on any device, any platform, anywhere, including IoT. It has features like **Automatic Speech Recognition (ASR)**, Global Vocabulary, Streaming Recognition, Word Hints, Real-Time Audio support, Noise Robustness, Inappropriate Content Filtering and supports for integration with other APIs of GCP.

The architecture of the Cloud Speech API is as follows:

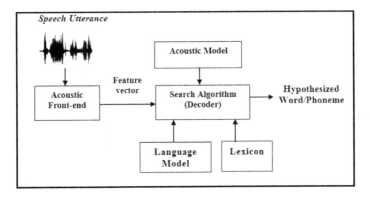

In other words, this model enables speech to text conversion by ML.

The components used by the Speech API are:

- REST API or **Google Remote Procedure Call (gRPC)** API
- Google Cloud Client Library
- JSON API
- Python
- Cloud DataLab
- Cloud Data Storage
- Cloud Endpoints

The applications of the model include:

- Voice user interfaces
- Domotic appliance control

- Preparation of structured documents
- Aircraft / direct voice outputs
- Speech to text processing
- Telecommunication

 It is free of charge for 15 seconds per usage, up to 60 minutes per month. More than that will be charged at $0.006 per usage.

Now, as we have learned about the concepts and the applications of the model, let's learn some use cases where we can implement the model:

- **Solving crimes with voice recognition**: **AGNITIO**, A voice biometrics specialist partnered with Morpho (Safran) to bring Voice ID technology into its multimodal suite of criminal identification products.
- **Buying products and services with the sound of your voice**: Another most popular and mainstream application of biometrics in general is mobile payments. Voice recognition has also made its way into this highly competitive arena.
- **A hands-free AI assistant that knows who you are**: Any mobile phone nowadays has voice recognition software in the form AI machine learning algorithms.

How to use Speech API - Video

Below is the link to the video which you can use to see how this given service is used.

Link: `https://www.youtube.com/watch?v=0bvN3H9jm_s`

QR code:

Cloud Translation API

Natural language processing (**NLP**) is a part of artificial intelligence that focuses on **Machine Translation** (**MT**). MT has become the main focus of NLP group since many years. MT deals with translating text in source language to text in target language. Cloud Translation API provides a graphical user interface to translate an inputted string of a language to targeted language, it's highly responsive, scalable and dynamic in nature. This API enables translation among 100+ languages. It also supports language detection automatically with accuracy. It provides a feature to read a web page contents and translate to another language, and need not be text extracted from a document. The Translation API supports various features such as programmatic access, text translation, language detection, continuous updates and adjustable quota, and affordable pricing.

The following image shows the architecture of the translation model:

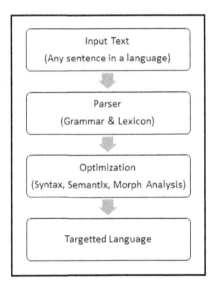

In other words, the cloud translation API is an adaptive Machine Translation algorithm.

The components used by this model are:

- REST API
- Cloud DataLab
- Cloud data storage

- Python, Ruby
- Clients Library
- Cloud Endpoints

The most important application of the model is conversion of a regional language to a foreign language.

 The cost of text translation and language detection is $20 per 1 million characters.

Use cases

Now, as we have learned about the concepts and applications of the API, let's learn two use cases where it has been successfully implemented:

- Rule-based Machine Translation
- Local Tissue Response to Injury and Trauma

We will discuss each of these use cases in the following sections.

Rule-based Machine Translation

The steps to implement rule based Machine Translation successfully are as follows:

1. Input text
2. Parsing
3. Tokenization
4. Compare the rules to extract meaning of prepositional phrase
5. Find word of inputted language to word of targeted language
6. Frame the sentence of targeted language

Local tissue response to injury and trauma

We can learn about the Machine Translation process from the responses of a local tissue to injuries and trauma. The human body follows a process similar to Machine Translation when dealing with injuries. We can roughly describe the process as follows:

1. Hemorrhaging from lesioned vessels and blood clotting
2. Blood-borne physiological components, leaking from the usually closed sanguineous compartment, are recognized as foreign material by the surrounding tissue since they are not tissue-specific
3. Inflammatory response mediated by macrophages (and more rarely by foreign-body giant cells)
4. Resorption of blood clot
5. Ingrowth of blood vessels and fibroblasts, and the formation of granulation tissue
6. Deposition of an unspecific but biocompatible type of repair (scar) tissue by fibroblasts

How to use Translation API - Video

Below is the link to the video which you can use to see how this given service is used.

Link: https://www.youtube.com/watch?v=cFo4l97d9A0

QR code:

Cloud Vision API

Cloud Vision API is powerful image analytic tool. It enables the users to understand the content of image. It helps in finding various attributes or categories of an image, such as labels, web, text, document, properties, safe search, and code of that image in JSON. In labels field there are many sub-categories like text, line, font, area, graphics, screenshots, and points. How much area of graphics involved, text percentage, what percentage of empty area and area covered by text, is there any image partially or fully mapped in web are included web contents. The document consists of blocks of image with detailed description, properties shows that the colors used in image is visualized. If any unwanted or inappropriate content is removed from the image through safe search. The main features of this API are label detection, explicit content detection, logo and landmark detection, face detection, web detection, and to extract the text the API used **Optical Character Reader** (**OCR**) and is supported for many languages. It does not support face recognition system.

The architecture for the Cloud Vision API is as follows:

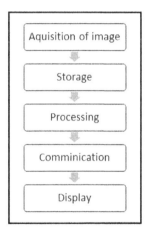

We can summarize the functionalities of the API as extracting quantitative information from images, taking the input as an image and the output as numerics and text.

The components used in the API are:

- Client Library
- REST API
- RPC API

- OCR Language Support
- Cloud Storage
- Cloud Endpoints

Applications of the API include:

- Industrial Robotics
- Cartography
- Geology
- Forensics and Military
- Medical and Healthcare

 Cost: Free of charge for the first 1,000 units per month; after that, pay as you go.

Use cases

This technique can be successfully implemented in:

- Image detection using an Android or iOS mobile device
- Retinal Image Analysis (Ophthalmology)

We will discuss each of these use cases in the following topics.

Image detection using Android or iOS mobile device

Cloud Vision API can be successfully implemented to detect images using your smartphone. The steps to do this are simple:

1. Input the image
2. Run the Cloud Vision API
3. Executes methods for detection of Face, Label, Text, Web and Document properties
4. Generate the response in the form of phrase or string
5. Populate the image details as a text view

Retinal Image Analysis – ophthalmology

Similarly, the API can also be used to analyze retinal images. The steps to implement this are as follows:

1. Input the images of an eye
2. Estimate the retinal biomarkers
3. Do the process to remove the effected portion without losing necessary information
4. Identify the location of specific structures
5. Identify the boundaries of the object
6. Find similar regions in two or more images
7. Quantify the image with retinal portion damage

How to use Vision API - Video

Below is the link to the video which you can use to see how this given service is used.

Link: https://www.youtube.com/watch?v=vMXoG33rn-E

QR code:

Cloud Video Intelligence

The content can easily search labels and discover within the entire video, shot by shot, or per frame. It allows us to identify automatically key points in video content with a massive recommendation library of 20,000 labels. It also returns confidence levels for each entity identified, so it can easily control and filter video content for what's most relevant. It provides insights on the changes that occurred in a scene or frame, and identifies appropriate locations (either regional or global) in videos to insert ads that are contextually relevant to the video content. It also automatically transcribes video content in English.

The architecture for Cloud Video Intelligence is as follows:

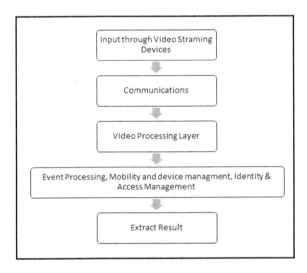

The core components used in this technique are:

- REST API
- RPC API
- Cloud Storage
- Cloud Endpoints
- Clients Library
- IAM

The API has found a variety of applications in:

- Aircraft
- Forensic science

- Automobiles
- Education
- Industry robotics
- Public transportation systems:
    - Eliminating overcrowding
    - Time management
    - Analyzing behavior
    - Ensuring safety
    - Detecting blind spots
    - Capturing incidents
- Security and surveillance system:
    - Video data collection
    - Processing engine
    - Data analytic engine
    - Log database
    - Extracting data and compare with existing
    - Report generation

 Regarding the pricing, the model has a pay-as-you-go process.

Dialogflow

Dialogflow is an API used to build interactive dialog box communications for mobile applications, websites and other platforms. It uses a natural language context intelligence API to provide quick responses to end users, based on what conversation it is. There are various prebuilt entities used to recognize a user's intent. It allows the users to build native server-less applications on an integrated code editor; it can be deployed on cloud or on premise. It supports user interaction conversations for cross-platform and as well as multilingual through text and voice. This has separate SLAs and ToS for standard and enterprise editions.

The architecture of Dialogflow is as follows:

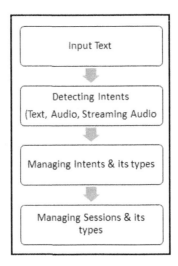

The main purpose of this model is to build user interfaces to interact between users and devices of various platforms, through text and voice.

The core components used in this model are:

- NLP API
- REST API
- RPC API
- Cloud Endpoints
- Cloud Speech API
- Cloud Storage
- Clients Library
- IoT API
- Cloud Function for Firebase

The model has found a variety of applications in:

- Digital commerce
- Telecommunication
- IoT
- Automobiles

The model is free for the standard edition, and you pay as you go for the enterprise edition.

Use cases

To learn more about this model, let's look at the following use cases:

- **Interactive Voice Response System (IVRS)** customer service
- Checkout free shopping

In the following sections, we will learn how we implement the Dialogflow model to successfully execute the use cases.

Interactive Voice Response System customer service

IVR, as we all know, allows customers to interact with a company's host system via text or by voice. We can enable this service when a user inquired about through the IVR dialog, as the person gets the response from IVR. IVR systems can be used for ticket booking, banking payments and services, retail orders, utilities, travel information, lodging complaints, and more.

Checkout free shopping

In self-driving cars, computer vision, sensor fusion, and deep learning are used. Similarly, a checkout-free shopping experience is made possible by the same types of technology. Automatically detecting when products are taken from the shelves or returned to the shelves, it keeps track of them in a virtual cart. When you're done shopping, you can just leave the store. Soon after that, you'll receive a receipt and will be charged from your associated bank account.

AutoML

The entire Cloud AutoML platform will help businesses scale up their AI capabilities without requiring advanced machine learning expertise. AutoML enables the end user to experience in learning high-quality NN models. Cloud AutoML Vision is built on GCP transfer learning and neural architecture search technologies. It is a simple, secure, and flexible ML API. Cloud AutoML provides a simple **graphical user interface (GUI)** to train, evaluate, improve, and deploy models. It is integrated easily with all other APIs of GCP.

The architecture of AutoML is as follows:

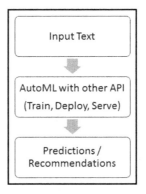

The core components used in the model are:

- Cloud Storage
- Cloud Dataflow
- Cloud Vision API
- Cloud Image API
- REST API
- RPC API
- Cloud Endpoints
- BigQuery/BigTable

The applications of this model include:

- Animation and gaming
- Digital Commerce
- Conservation of animals and their habits (London Zoo)
- Recommendation systems

- Healthcare and medical
- Automobiles
- Home appliances

 This method follows a pay-as-you-go pricing policy for its services.

Use case – Listening to music by fingerprinting

The Cloud AutoML platform can be used to implement a wide array of functionalities, such as listening to music with fingerprints. It is a technique to toggle and play music and audio clips with using your fingerprints. The steps to execute this technique are as follows:

1. Take input as a music signal
2. Convert it into samples and design a spectrogram
3. Find the peak point of the signal
4. Hash fingerprinting
5. Learn new songs and listen to unknown songs from the database
6. Align and compress the music

Summary

In this chapter, we learned about artificial intelligence and how it can be applied to day-to-day problems. We also learned about machine learning techniques and related APIs, which helped us to address and ease common scenarios. We looked at some real-life use cases, where we implemented the techniques hands-on.

In the next chapter, we will be learning something that will take our knowledge and skills to the next level—troubleshooting mechanisms.

7

Guidance on Google Cloud Platform Certification

So far, we have learned about all the major components that the Google Cloud Platform has to offer. Having knowledge is a great thing, but implementing the skills that you have attained is the more vital aspect in the industry. And certifications are very helpful. While they test your knowledge on specific tools, they also check whether you have architectural knowledge of the platform. Thus, I am writing this chapter to focus on the certification part of Google Cloud Platform, a small guidance chapter that will be helpful for you to crack the certification.

Google Cloud Platform offers two certifications, divided into Architecture and Data Engineer. The topics that we are going to cover in this chapter are:

- Exam guide for Professional Cloud Architect Certification
- Exam guide for Professional Data Engineer Certification
- When to use what

Professional Cloud Architect Certification

The following is the list of services that are typically expected to be known in order to become a Professional Cloud Architect.

Topics for cloud architect certification

The following are the list of important topics required for the certification:

- Cloud virtual network
- Google compute engine
- Cloud IAM
- Data storage services
- Resource management
- Interconnecting network and load balancing
- Autoscaling
- Infrastructure automation with Cloud API and deployment manager
- Managed services
- Application infra services
- Application development services
- Containers

Let's discuss all of them in more detail.

Cloud virtual network

In Cloud virtual network, the major components are understanding projects, networks, and subnetworks. In GCP, we have *Projects* to distinguish between different accounts. In the same way, you need to understand the concepts of working of addresses, routes, and rules. This will help you clear the fundamentals in networking, which are vital going ahead with Google Cloud Platform.

Google Compute Engine

In Google Compute Engine, the focus is mainly on working with virtual machines in GCP. In this, you need some good hands-on experience with respect to starting the instance, and selecting the right compute options, images, and different disk options that GCP has to offer. The utility of each Compute Engine will vary with respect to the use case. So, have a good understanding of that!

Cloud IAM

Cloud Identity and Access Management, or **Cloud IAM**, has a vital role to play with respect to access management in GCP. Get a very good understanding of organization, roles, members, and service accounts. Understand the *Principle of Least Privilege* while assigning the roles.

Data Storage Services

In data storage services, we have many services such as Cloud Storage, Cloud SQL, Cloud Spanner, Datastore, Bigtable, and BigQuery. Questions are often asked like this: with a given scenario, what should be the right service to choose? For example, we have a scenario where the data source is files and they are documents of a team loading the data to GCP. We have to choose the current Data Storage Service. In this scenario, the best option would be Cloud Storage, as it can store data in object format. Similarly, if you want a SQL-like engine but the requirement is strong consistency and high availability, you are left with two options: Cloud SQL and Cloud Spanner. Cloud Spanner will be a better option over Cloud SQL due to the provision of strong consistency and high availability.

Resource management and resource monitoring

This is a small topic considering the depth of GCP. In resource management, the questions asked can be around the different ways in which you can manage your cloud. So, a few options can be using quotas and assigning the right labels and names.

In resource monitoring, it is mostly about stackdriver. We know by now that we have stackdriver monitoring, stackdriver logging, error reporting, tracing, and debugging. It can be very confusing sometimes to understand the right purpose of each tool.

Interconnecting network and load balancing

This part is more about virtual private network, cloud interconnect, and direct peering. With these three interconnection options, you can have an optimum solution in your architecture.

Load balancing has multiple solutions, such as internet, internal, single region, multiple regions, and so on. You can also have a rule-based routing mechanism, content-based load balancing, and cross-region load balancing.

Also, get a good understanding of the best practices in load balancing for certification.

Autoscaling

Autoscaling is available as part of the Compute Engine API, but the restriction is that it is for managed instance groups. Also understand that in case of a zone failure or if a group of instances fails, 33% or one-third of the capacity is lost; but the remaining capacity is still there in other zones. The Autoscaler moving window is very fast—just 1 min. Autoscaler moving window means how fast autoscaling can be enabled by initiating more instances.

Infrastructure automation with Cloud API and Deployment Manager

Now, as an architect, you have a clear idea about the infrastructure, the right option with respect to a suitable service for a scenario, and many other aspects. Then, we can start automating infrastructure deployment. And we have two ways to do so—using Cloud API and Deployment Manager.

To use Cloud API, you need to download the Cloud SDK. By using this Cloud SDK, you can use Go, Java, Python, Node.js, PHP, Ruby, and C#; all are supported. This is a terminal-based service by GCP.

`gcloud`, `gsutil`, `bq`, and `kubectl` are some of the CLI tools.

Now, over to Deployment Manager. This is more of a orchestration tool. Very powerful and has many features! If you have worked on Deployment Manager, Puppet, Chef, or Cloud Formation, then Deployment Manager is easy to learn.

We can create a template in yaml and deploy.

Try some hands-on work with this and that should be okay to go with.

Managed services

Cloud infrastructure, as we all know, is divided into IaaS, PaaS, and SaaS. Managed services fall under PaaS and SaaS services. So, the major managed services in GCP are Dataproc, Dataflow, and BigQuery.

Get a complete understanding of Dataproc, Dataflow, and BigQuery; perform some hands-on work and you should get a clear idea about it.

Other services that you should be aware of also include Cloud Datalab and Google Data Studio.

Application infra services

In application infrastructure services, we have services that are common for applications and systems. This includes Cloud Pub/Sub, API Management, Cloud Functions, Cloud Source Repositories, and a few specialty APIs.

Read more about these services, the different features they offer, and their different use cases.

Application development services

Under Application Development Services, we have Google App Engine. We have two variations of Google App Engine: standard and flexible. The major difference between them is support for languages, with flexible obviously having more support.

Containers

This topic is focused on various container options that GCP provides us: Google Container Engine (Kubernetes) and Google Container Registry. Understand the difference between them and you are ready to go.

Job role description

In this section, we are going to discuss the things expected from a Cloud Architect. So, as a Cloud Architect, you are expected to help companies make the most of GCP services. You need to provide your inputs in designing, managing, and developing a secure, highly available infrastructure. In short, you are expected to know about all the important services in Google Cloud Platform. If you have worked on a hybrid cloud or some other cloud platform, it will be a huge plus to understand and work with GCP.

Other things that you need to be aware of are designing a solution for business requirement, infrastructure requirements meeting technical requirements, controlling network and storage, creating a migration plan, and meeting future aspects of the design.

The next expectation is about managing and assisting in providing solutions in infrastructure. This includes configuring network topologies and configuring storage systems. Other major aspects are security, compliance, and analyzing and optimizing technical business processes.

Certification preparation

Cloud Architect certification is 120 minutes in duration and costs $200. GCP has provided four use cases and you can expect questions related to those use cases only. I have shared these use cases in the next topic. Practicing on Qwiklabs (`https://qwiklabs.com`) will be a great plus to you. Read in detail about the documentations as well. This is the expected preparation you can go with.

The certification questions focus mainly on scenario-based questions. Under GCP certification, they will be asking you about a scenario or requirement that a company has, and you are supposed to choose the right option in it. Sometimes, it might also happen that you will have to choose multiple options.

You will also find some simple questions that won't take more than 10 seconds to answer, but they are very few in number.

Sample questions

1. What data storage service would you select if you just need to migrate a standard relational database running on a single machine in a data center to the cloud?

- Cloud SQL
- BigQuery
- Persistent Disk
- Cloud Storage

2. What is the purpose of the Stackdriver Trace service?

- Reporting on latency as part of managing performance
- Reporting on GCP system errors
- Reporting on application errors
- Reporting on GCP resource consumption as part of managing performance

3. Why would you use Cloud Interconnect or Direct Peering rather than VPN?

- Cloud Interconnect and Direct Peering are cheaper because you can turn them on and off easily when not in use
- Google only offers SLAs for Cloud Interconnect and Direct Peering
- VPN does not offer control over IP address assignment and CIDR subnets, while Cloud Interconnect and Direct Peering do

- Cloud Interconnect and Direct Peering can provide higher availability, lower latency, and lower cost for data-intensive applications

4. Go to the Dress4Win case study here and review: `https://cloud.google.com/certification/guides/cloud-architect/casestudy-dress4win`. Then proceed to answer the question.

Dress4Win has both a Hadoop ecosystem and a Spark system provisioned in house. Now they are opting to migrate their Big Data Solutions to a cloud that is managed, fast, and scalable. What would be the best solution for this?

- Cloud DataFlow
- Cloud Datalab
- Cloud Spanner
- Cloud DataProc

5. Go to the JencoMart case study here and review: `https://cloud.google.com/certification/guides/cloud-architect/casestudy-jencomart`. Then proceed to answer the question.

The first task they want to perform is migration of PostSQL databases to GCP, assuming that the target service would support their non-relational database. Make a point that this would also need to be a managed service with support to encryption.

What GCP solution would you advise them to use to migrate PostSQL to?

- BigTable
- BigQuery
- Cloud SQL
- Cloud Spanner

Use cases

Read thoroughly about the following use cases. You will surely find at least one of them in the certification exam:

- Jenco Mart: `https://cloud.google.com/certification/guides/cloud-architect/casestudy-jencomart`
- Mountkirk Games: `https://cloud.google.com/certification/guides/cloud-architect/casestudy-mountkirkgames`

- **Dress4Win:** `https://cloud.google.com/certification/guides/cloud-architect/casestudy-dress4win`
- **Terram Earth:** `https://cloud.google.com/certification/guides/cloud-architect/casestudy-terramearth`

You can learn more about Architect Certification from below links:

- List of all certification Google offers - `https://cloud.google.com/certification`
- Official Google Training - `https://cloud.google.com/training`
- GCP Cloud Architect - `https://cloud.google.com/certification/cloud-architect`

All the best!! :)

Professional Data Engineer Certification

Up next is the list of services that are typically a must-know for a Professional Data Engineer.

Topics for Cloud Data Engineer Certification

The following are the list of important topics required for the certification:

- BigQuery
- Dataflow
- Dataproc
- Machine Learning API
- TensorFlow
- Stream Pipeline
- Streaming Analytics and Dashboards

Let's discuss all of them in more detail.

BigQuery

BigQuery, as we know by now, is a serverless SQL data analysis tool on petabyte-scale data. Have some very good hands-on experience on the service and study different use cases. Learn how BigQuery works and the features it supports: serverlessness, SQL-like queries, wildcards, loading data (using a CLI, web UI, or API).

You can also have a user-defined function and the different constraints it has. Learn a few best practices such as stopping projecting unnecessary columns, filtering often with the where cause, and many others.

Dataflow

As you already know by now, Dataflow is about autoscaling the data processing pipeline on GCP. You can ingest, transform, and load data in one go. If you have worked on Apache Beam, it will be a good plus. Java and Python have very good support for Dataflow. Experiment with aggregation, combine, and `group by`.

Dataproc

Dataproc, in simple terms, is Hadoop on cloud. In Dataproc, understand how to create a cluster, different types of clusters, using pre-emptible workers to save money, and many other features.

And how you utilize it will be a sole responsibility of yours.

For Dataproc, you can have Cloud Dataproc, BigQuery, Cloud Storage, Cloud Bigtable, and Compute Engine as an input. While you can have Cloud Dataproc, BigQuery, Cloud Storage, Cloud BigTable, Compute Engine as output.

Machine Learning API and TensorFlow

Machine Learning is a very important aspect of today's world. GCP provides us with two options in Machine Learning: custom ML models and pre-trained ML models.

In custom ML models, we have Tensorflow and Machine Learning Engine; whereas in pre-trained ML models, we have Vison API, Speech API, Jobs API, Translation API, and Natural Language API.

Do some experiments with these things and you will get a very good understanding of the same. But for this, you require a good knowledge of machine learning.

Tensorflow is important in many aspects; that's why it is important to understand Tensorflow in great detail.

Stream Pipeline, Streaming Analytics, and Dashboards

Stream processing can have a few questions; understand the flow of data in an architecture, such as Cloud Pub/Sub, Cloud Dataflow, BigTable, and Google BigQuery.

Apache Beam and Cloud Dataflow are other tools associated with streaming. Again, experiment with them!! Google Data Studio can be used for a dashboard; it is basic in stage. But you cannot deny of not having question in certification based on Data Studio.

Job role description

Now we are going to discuss the things expected from a Data Engineer. As a Cloud Data Engineer, you will be helping companies in the implementation of strategies. From troubleshooting to maintaining to building and designing, your input will be required.

As a data engineer, you are also bound to implement the reliability, security, fault tolerance, and efficiency of such systems.

You have to work with designing data processing systems; data pipeline; data processing infrastructure; and building a good data structure, strategies, and databases. Building and maintaining data pipelines and processing infrastructure can be also counted. Then there is analyzing data, implementing machine learning models, modeling business use cases, and ensuring reliability.

Now that you are done with analyzing, it's time to work on visualizing and advocating policy. And one thing a data engineer is obviously expected to have a good understanding of is security and compliance designing.

Certification preparation

Cloud Data Engineer certification is also 120 minutes in duration and costs 200$. GCP has provided two use cases and you can expect questions related to those use cases only. I have shared these use cases in the next topic. Practicing on Qwiklabs (`https://qwiklabs.com`) will be a great plus to you. Read the documentation in detail as well. This is the expected preparation you can go with.

The certification questions focus mainly on codes. Under GCP certification, they will be asking you about a scenario or requirement that a company has, and you are supposed to choose the right option. Sometimes, it might also happen that you will have to choose multiple options.

You will also find some simple questions that won't take more than 10 seconds to answer, but they are very few in number.

Sample questions

1. How does the autoscaler resolve conflicts between multiple scaling policies?

- First come, first served
- It selects the one that recommends the most VMs to ensure that the application is supported
- It selects the one with the fewest VMs to provide the lowest cost
- It is based on priority, a value set in each policy that determines the precedence

2. `gsutil mb gs://mike_bucket_100`: this command will delete a bucket called `gs://mike_bucket_100`.

- True
- False

3. Which of these is correct about the code `datalab create nyc32`?

- It creates a new dataproc instance
- It creates a new datalab instance called datalabvm
- It creates a new datalab instance called nyc32

4. On all MySQL instances, autoscaling is on by default.

- True
- False

5. Go to the MJTelco case study at `https://cloud.google.com/certification/guides/data-engineer/casestudy-mjtelco`. Then proceed to answer the question.

They have a use case of handling telemetry data. Data is generated in real time and it is often tough to handle this huge data. The requirement is to handle this data, analyze it on the go, and load it into a SQL-supported analytics engine. One thing you must take care of is that the data is in JSON format and you have to convert it into text format on the go. Choose the name and sequence of tools you will be developing on:

- Cloud Pub/Sub; Compute Engine; Cloud SQL
- Cloud Pub/Sub; Cloud Dataflow; BigQuery
- Cloud Storage; Cloud Dataflow; BigQuery
- Cloud Storage; Compute Engine; Cloud SQL

Use cases

Read thoroughly about the following use cases. You will surely find at least one of them in your certification exam:

- Flowlogistic: `https://cloud.google.com/certification/guides/data-engineer/casestudy-flowlogistic`
- MJTelco: `https://cloud.google.com/certification/guides/data-engineer/casestudy-mjtelco`

You can learn more about Data Engineer Certification from below links:

- List of all certification Google offers: `https://cloud.google.com/certification`
- Official Google Training: `https://cloud.google.com/training`
- GCP Cloud Data Engineer: `https://cloud.google.com/certification/data-engineer`

All the best!! :)

When to use What

In this topic I will be sharing some diagrammatic images to help you in getting the right understanding of which service to use in which situation. This will be very helpful for you.

Choosing Cloud Storage

Confused when to use Cloud Storage, have a look at the following flow diagram:

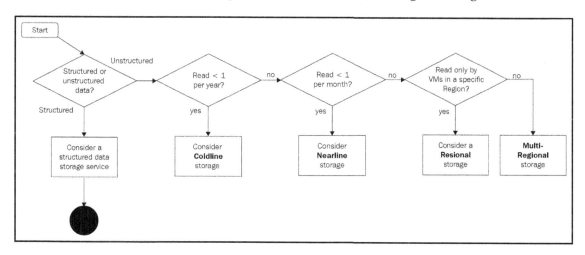

Choosing Cloud SQL

Confused when to use Cloud SQL, have a look at the following flow diagram:

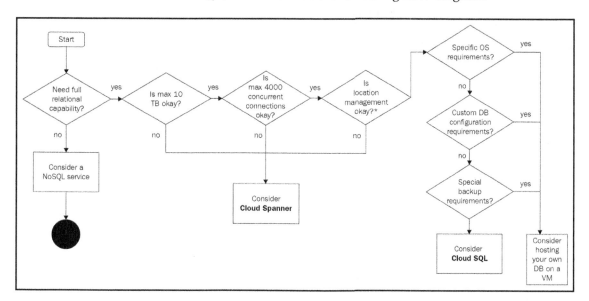

Choosing Cloud Spanner

Confused when to use Cloud Spanner, have a look at the following flow diagram:

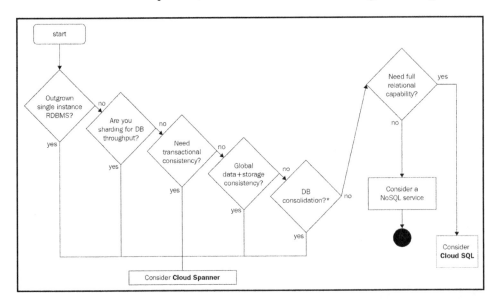

Choosing DataStore

Confused when to use Cloud Datastore, have a look at the following flow diagram:

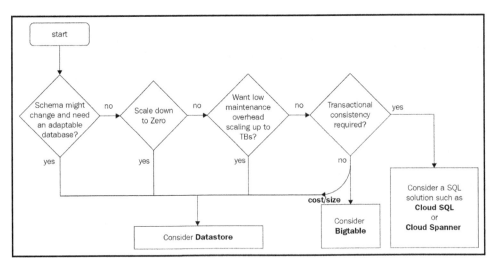

Choosing BigTable

Confused when to use Cloud BigTable, have a look at the following flow diagram:

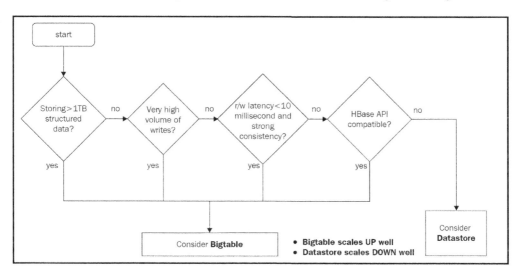

Choosing right data storage

Maybe other way of looking into the overall data storage options we have and which to choose when, below diagram to help you with that.

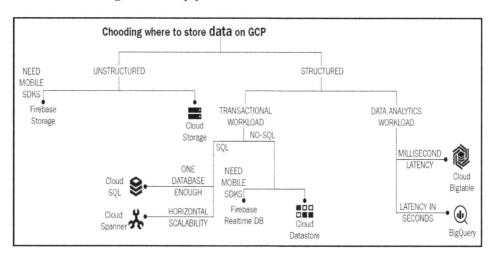

Dataproc versus Dataflow

Confused as when to use Dataproc and when to use Dataflow? Below is the answer.

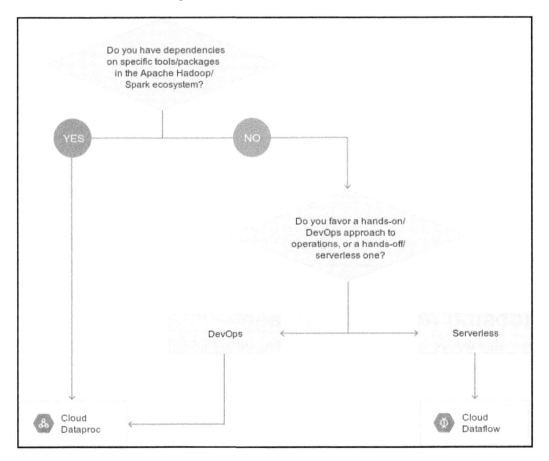

Data Peering versus Carrier Peering versus IPSec VPN versus Dedicated Interconnect

A helpful diagram for understanding when to go for Data Peering, Carrier Peering, IPSec VPN and Dedicated Interconnect.

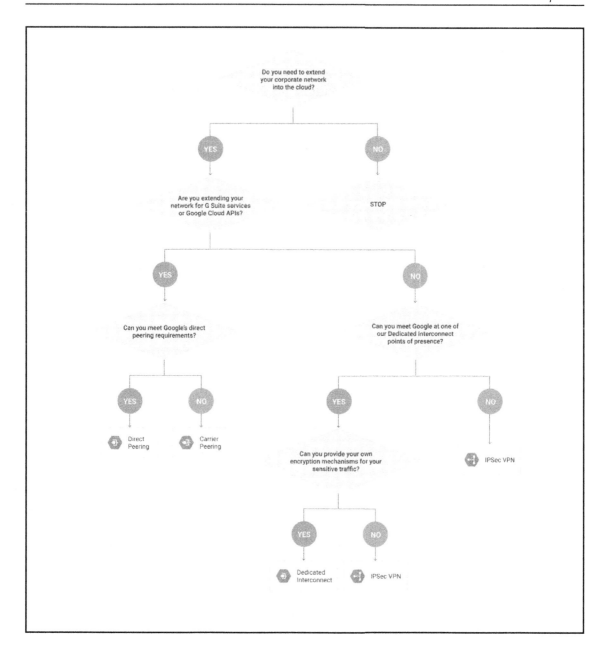

Summary

With this chapter, you might have got a complete idea of the way you can prepare to clear your Google Cloud Platform certifications for Professional Cloud Architect and Professional Data Engineer.

The next chapter will help you in a great way to get a complete understanding of the different use cases that we have respect to GCP. We will be studying three different use cases. See you there!!

8
Business Use Cases

We have now reached our last chapter. I hope that by now you have a great understanding of all the services, tools, and products that **Google Cloud Platform (GCP)** has to offer. I have tried my best to explain each and every component of GCP and how it works. I hope that you have enjoyed going through the book.

The next thing that we will be focusing on is business use cases. Right now you have a very good understanding of all the services that GCP offers us, but how they fit into the project is still a bit tough to understand. So the main aim of this chapter is to give you the required end to end knowledge of any typical project in Google Cloud Platform.

Therefore, this chapter will help you to gain a complete understanding of a few different use cases. The use cases are divided into multiple parts. Each use case will start with two lines about the use case. Next is an introduction, in the introduction I will be explaining about the use case, the domain of the project, and some more information at a superficial level.

The third part will be the problem, what is the problem that they are facing. Because not every company moves onto cloud in the first go. So we will discuss the problems that they are facing with respect to current infrastructure.

In the fourth step we will identify and brainstorm all the services that will be required for the project. And then I will jot down the list of all tools that we will be utilizing in step five.

The sixth step will be building a draft architecture of the project - remember this will be a draft architecture, many changes can be expected in the architecture.

And we will end the use case with a conclusion.

If you have gone through my bio, you should be aware of the fact that I am an entrepreneur as well as a consultant and corporate trainer. As an entrepreneur, I am building a product by the name of Mark N Park to help customers find parking vacancies in real time.

So, the first use case is my product Mark N Park on Google Cloud Platform.

The second use case is based on TensorFlow and Web Mining Recommendations.

And the third use case will be building an analytics engine and Data Lake on the top of GCP. We will have a good look at this use case, while understanding numerous services of GCP.

The following are the use cases we are going to study:

- Smart Parking Solution by Mark N Park
- DSS for Web Mining Recommendation using TensorFlow
- Building Data Lake for a Telecom Client

Smart Parking Solution by Mark N Park

This use case is going to focus more on the IoT and data processing side of the application.

Abstract

In this use case, our aim is to find real-time parking occupancy of four wheel vehicles and show it on mobile and web apps.

Introduction

Now with the introduction and abstract you have already got an idea of the use cases. But this will be in more detail. So, we have to build an application on Google Cloud Platform where our primary aim is to show the real-time occupancy of vehicle parking.

And to show the real-time occupancy of the parking lots we require that information to be updated in the database. For this purpose we have multiple options, such as installing numerous cameras covering the entire parking lot. Another option can be installing GPS locating sensors to every vehicle entering the premise. And one more option can be installing sensors that detect the presence and absence of vehicles in the parking lot.

Let's assume we are going with option number three, that is installing sensors. Thus, now we have sensors installed across all parking spaces. But to receive data from the sensor we need some Wi-Fi or LiFi or GSM module installed at the location.

Considering we have any of these mechanism installed, they will start transmitting data across the network using it. Now we are receiving data at our designated service. The data that we are receiving needs to be analyzed, processed, and transmitted to the interface device—web app and mobile application.

And from there the user can access the real-time occupancy of the parking space.

Problems

Now that you are very clear with respect to the use case, let's discuss different challenges that we might face with respect to the use case.

So, the sensors are recording data and transmitting in real time. We do not have the option of locally storing the data. This data needs to be directed to the cloud directly. But where on the cloud? There are multiple options for catching this data sent by sensors.

We have received the data from millions of sensors. The next task is categorizing it, because the data is coming from multiple locations and we have to make sure that data is updated for the right location. Since we have the data now it is very important to show it in the right format. While this data is displayed to the end customer, at the same time we also want to get reports and show a dashboard for business analysis.

While we are discussing all the challenges, scaling can also be considered a huge concern while adding new sensors on the system.

Thus the challenges are:

- Collection of sensor data in real time
- Updating the right dataset/database
- Storing periodic data
- Transmitting the data to the end user
- Reports and dashboard output required
- Scaling infrastructure

With so many challenges, in the next section we will try to brainstorm which different Google Cloud Platform Services we can utilize.

Brainstorming

Considering the challenges that we have listed previously, we will now do some brain storm surrounding it.

Collection of sensor data in real time

The data that sensors transmit is either though TCP/IP (HTTP) or through MQTT protocol. When we are dealing with the data that is coming from HTTP or MQTT, the best solution is using Google Cloud IoT Core. Google Cloud IoT Core helps us to collect the data across sensors and scale automatically.

Updating the right dataset/database

Once the data is received, our next task is to update the right dataset. Google IoT Core publishes the data to Cloud Pub/Sub. Now, once Cloud Pub/Sub has the data, we can store it as per our will and destination.

Storing periodic data

Using Cloud Pub/Sub we can store the data in Cloud Dataflow, Cloud BigQuery, or Cloud Bigtable.

Transmitting the data to the end user

To show data to the customers we can use the existing APIs or we can custom build our APIs. These APIs can be then connected to Firebase as well. Firebase is a Database as a Service product bought by Google. Thus, Android, iOS, and web apps can be connected to Firebase.

Reports and dashboard output required

Depending on where the data is stored, you can create your reports and dashboards. For reporting purposes, we can also use Google Data Studio.

Scaling infrastructure

Most of the services that we have mentioned earlier are fully managed, so no user involvement is required.

Services

Therefore, if I consider the services that I might be using for this use case, they will be as follows:

- Cloud IoT Core
- Cloud Pub/Sub
- Cloud Dataflow
- Cloud Bigtable
- Cloud BigQuery
- Google Data Studio
- Apigee API Platform
- Cloud Endpoints

Architecture

The high level architecture for the given use case is shown as follows:

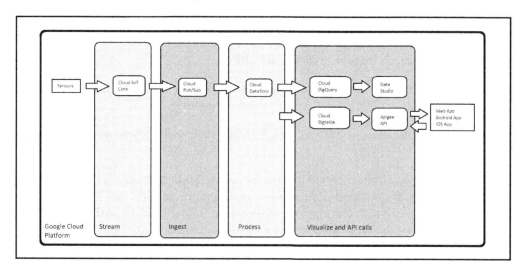

Conclusion

And thus we can conclude that the Smart Parking solution requires numerous tools to stream, ingest, process, and visualize data.

DSS for web mining recommendation using TensorFlow

This use case is going to focus more on using TensorFlow and doing Web Mining on GCP.

Abstract

Decision supports systems (DSSs) are computer-based information systems designed to help managers to select one of the many alternative solutions to a problem. Web mining is the application of data mining techniques to discover patterns from the **World Wide Web**. The aim of this use case is to find patterns to recommend to users using TensorFlow.

Introduction

A brief idea of the use case is presented in the abstract. Now the detailed part of the use case is as follows in the corresponding sections. We have to build an application on Google Cloud Platform where the aim of the use case is shown as recommended systems.

Decision support system (DSS) is a computer-based information system that supports business or organizational decision-making activities.

Recommender systems (RS) aim to capture the user behavior by suggesting/recommending users with relevant items or services that they find interesting.

Web mining is the application of data mining techniques to extract knowledge from web data.

TensorFlow is an open source software library for numerical computation using dataflow graphs. Deep learning in the cloud platform is a new type of service facilitated by all cloud platforms. This service can use TensorFlow in Google Cloud Platform and it enables users to develop a quick and easy way of application design, development, and deployment.

Problems

Web data is a combination of web content, web structure, and web usage. The content may be any two or more combinations of text, images, audio, videos, files, and so on. The structure is hyperlinks, tags, and so on, and the usage may be protocol data or logs, server logs, and other log records.

The following challenges are faced when accessing this type of data:

- Internet bandwidth
- Local systems or mobile hardware configuration
- Collection of data in real time
- Updating the right database
- Storing periodic data
- Extracting the data to the end user
- Reports generation as per requirements of the end user
- Scaling infrastructure

A DSS is an interactive computer-based information system with an organized collection of models, people, procedures, software, databases, telecommunication, and devices, which helps decision makers to solve unstructured or semi-structured business problems.

Brainstorming

Considering the challenges that we have listed previously, we will do some brain storm surrounding them.

Internet bandwidth

On low speed internet, more time is taken to process data on the web. Therefore, it is suggested to have high speed internet.

Local systems or mobile hardware configuration

There should be a common platform for representing of semi-structured or unstructured data. An easy architecture provides computation to one or more CPUs such as desktop, server, and mobile device with an API of TensorFlow.

Collection of data in real time

To transfer the data through HTTPS, collect the data across a distributed network with various structures of networks. The dataset API has a mechanism to create, load, and perform operations on data.

Updating the right database

A dataset contains structured elements, the shapes and types of the dataset take on the same structure. This dataset contains dictionaries of scalars, which all types of data can store.

Storing periodic data

We will be storing data streamed from Cloud Pub/Sub service to any one of these services - Cloud Dataflow or Cloud BigQuery or Cloud Bigtable.

Extracting the data to the end user

Existing APIs are used to transmit the data. The API can easily connect any type of the device, as desktop or mobile.

Report generation as per requirements of the end user

Through Google Data Studio or Estimators, we can generate the results in the form of automatic generated graphs.

Scaling of infrastructure

Most services are scalable and fully manageable, thus we don't need to manage these services manually.

Services

The services that I might be using for this use case are as follows:

- Cloud TensorFlow
- Cloud Pub/Sub

- Cloud Dataflow
- Cloud Bigtable
- Cloud BigQuery
- Google Data Studio
- Apigee API Platform
- Cloud Endpoints

Architecture

The following is an architectural diagram that gives a conceptual framework showing the flow of a sequence use case:

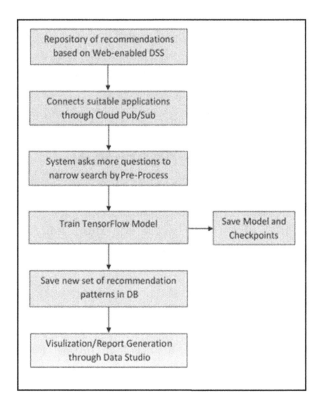

The following diagram explains in detail the internal flow of data to generate a new set of recommendations:

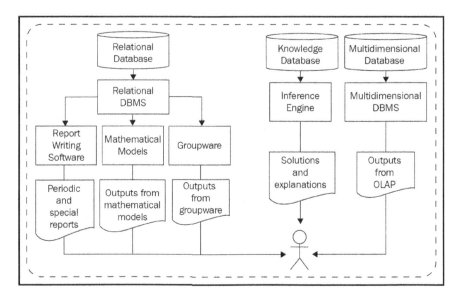

Advantages of using TensorFlow

It has an intuitive construct, because as the name suggests, it has a *flow of tensors*. You can easily visualize each and every part of the graph:

- Easily train on the CPU/GPU for distributed computing.
- Platform flexibility. You can run models wherever you want, whether it is on mobile, server, or PC.

Limitations of TensorFlow

Even though TensorFlow is powerful, it's still a low level library. For example, it can be considered as a machine level language, which needs modularity and high level interface through the frameworks, such as Keras:

- It's still in development, so much more awesomeness to come

- It depends on your hardware specs, the more the merrier
- Still not an API for many languages

There are still many things yet to be included in TensorFlow, such as OpenCL support.

Conclusion

The use case *DSS for Web Mining Recommendation using TensorFlow* uses the TensorFlow Machine Learning algorithm services of Google Cloud Platform, which helps users to get recommendations efficiently and effectively in less time.

Building a Data Lake for a Telecom Client

This use case is going to focus more on the analytics engine and building a Data Lake on cloud.

Abstract

A telecom company requires a to build a Data Lake on cloud and build an analytics engine on the top of that.

Introduction

The telecom project comprises building a Data Lake as well as data migration for a 25 years old telecom company. The client is a renowned telecom company and has a good presence in Asia, Europe, Africa, and some parts of North America. Their customer base is widely spread across India, Bangladesh, African countries, Latin America, and Middle-Eastern countries. The data resides in various data sources, more than 205. The data includes customer data (even secured), customer location data, tower locations for specific geographies, customer care complaints, feedback, and many other types of data.

Data is in CSV, PSV, TEXT, MSG, audio files, XML, JSON, and even in RDBMS (MySQL, Sybase, Oracle) databases in structured format.

The first task was to build a Data Lake on Google Cloud Platform and the second was to ingest data.

The project is divided into two stages, which we will discuss in the following section.

Problems

We will now discuss the first task—building a Data Lake. In `Chapter 4`, *Ingestion and Storing*, and `Chapter 5`, *Processing and Visualizing*, you have already been given an idea of all required tools that will be helping us in building a Data Lake.

So, the main purpose of a Data Lake is for storing a huge amount of data in one place. This is done to pull data as per our requirement for different use cases in organizations.

So, as we are building the Data Lake we need to understand the different types of data that will be dumped into a Data Lake. Volume, velocity, and variety - all three Vs need to be considered. Data as we know is in the form of files, images, and emails. It can also come in the form of server logs from many servers and databases. We have a total of 205 data sources; 107 are files, 93 are RDBMS, and 5 are live data sources

Under these circumstances, we cannot have just one mechanism to handle all the data that is being dumped. Thus, infrastructure should handle stream, batch, and unstructured data - that too at scale. In phase one we are only concentrating on accumulating the data. The data is coming as it is and we are not making any changes in it such as processing or analyzing. The data just needs to be categorized accurately on the basis of its source.

Thus from the previous discussions we can conclude that in this phase the following are the challenges:

- Identify source type (Batch or RDBMS or Stream)
- Logging was carriedout and logs were created for every file that was covered
- RDBMS import to create files automatically for MySQL and Postgres
- Ingesting live data into GCP
- Destination different for all the data sources
- Code repository

The following figure shows the 205 Data Sources and Data Lake:

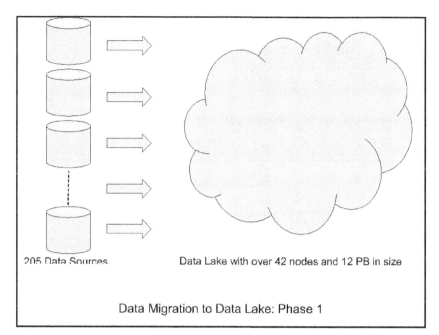

205 Data Sources

Data Lake with over 42 nodes and 12 PB in size

Data Migration to Data Lake: Phase 1

Now for the second task - to pull data from the Data Lake and clean it. The data on a Data Lake needs to be identified first before pulling it in for different use cases in organizations - such as finding a fraudulent customer. Therefore, the **business analyst (BA)** team identifies the data sources that they can leverage. Here again some part of data ingestion tools was required, but this time as we are using Hadoop clusters we can use the Hadoop ecosystem to perform the same task.

Once the data source is identified by BAs then a technical team will perform the task of dumping it into a Hadoop cluster. Once the data is cleaned and mapped - analytics was supposed to be performed on the data and in the last stage it should represent it in the form of reports and visualization. We can also run machine learning algorithms on this data.

So the following are the challenges with phase 2:

- Building a Hadoop Cluster
- Data ingestion prioritization and then ingestion
- Building strict policies between the Data Lake and Hadoop cluster users
- Maintaining a high availability, enabled load balancer, auto scaled, and secured cluster

- Maintain Cluster health
- Alpha phase is bringing data from the Data Lake into the application cluster
- Beta phase includes cleaning data
- Gamma phase performs transformations
- Delta phase graphs and reports are generated on multiple BI tools
- Code repository

The following figure shows us how we are pulling data from the Data Lake to our analytics engine:

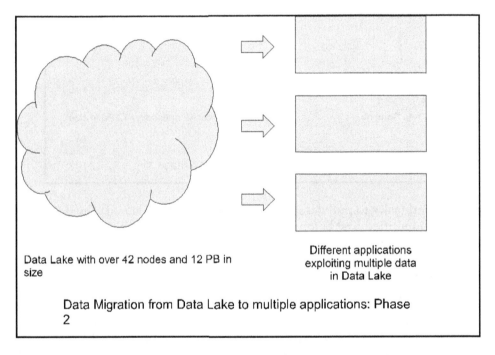

Data Lake with over 42 nodes and 12 PB in size

Different applications exploiting multiple data in Data Lake

Data Migration from Data Lake to multiple applications: Phase 2

We will discuss all these challenges in the following section.

Brainstorming

In the following section, we will discuss the challenges encountered from phase 1 and phase 2, respectively.

Challenges from phase 1

The following are the challenges from phase 1:

Identify source type (Batch or RDBMS or Stream)

First we have to identify the right source of the data to import. On the basis of the data source we have to identify the right tool to use. For streaming data we can either use Cloud Pub/Sub or Cloud Dataflow - if the data source is event-based and we do not require any processing, we can go for Cloud Pub/Sub.

If data is in batches in the form of file, we can use Cloud Storage to store this unstructured data in the form of objects. For this purpose we can use gsutil or Storage Transfer Service - depending on the source of data.

Logging was carried out and logs were created for every file that was covered

While we are ingesting data we also have to take care of all the logging. To handle the logging part we can use Stackdriver Logging. Stackdriver Logging is used to store, analyze, and monitor logging data. But we have to understand that this logging is predominantly for GCP services and not file logging as such.

RDBMS import to create files automatically for MySQL and Postgres

To import RDBMS data into Cloud SQL, we can use the mysqldump command. The primary destination of all this data will be Cloud SQL as of now.

Ingesting live data into GCP

Now, if we have the use case of ingesting live data then as we know we have two options - Cloud Pub/Sub and Cloud Dataflow. Cloud Pub/Sub is used when our data is event based and Cloud Dataflow is used when our data source requires some processing before dumping into GCP storage service.

Different destinations for all the data sources

Another challenge that we have listed down is different destinations of our data sources. Depending on the further utility of data, we can dump data either in Cloud Storage, Cloud Bigtable, or Cloud BigQuery.

Code repository

All the code that we are building requires us to store the code in a repository. For this purpose, we can use GCP's Cloud Source Repository.

Challenges from phase 2

The following are the challenges from phase 2.

Building Hadoop cluster

So, the data is currently stored in a Data Lake across multiple GCP services such as Cloud Storage, Cloud Bigtable, Cloud Bigquery, and so on. We also require a Hadoop cluster to perform some tasks. So, we can use Cloud Dataproc to start our own Hadoop cluster and utilize the Hadoop ecosystem.

Data ingestion prioritization and then ingestion

Now we know we have 200+ data sources dumped in the Data Lake - but we do not require all of them for this specific application. Therefore, we require the right data (Server Log data over RDBMS data) to be prioritized for ingestion.

Building strict policies between Data Lake and Hadoop cluster users

As we know we have different sets of teams working on the Data Lake and Hadoop cluster, therefore, using IAM roles we need to segregate the users and their privileges. We can control this by using right policies in Identity and Access Management.

Maintaining high availability, enabled load balancer, auto scaled, and secured cluster

The cluster can be accessed by numerous developers across the globe, therefore we need to maintain the high availability, load balancing, auto scaling, and security of the cluster. In this scenario, we have to make sure that we are using Cloud Load Balancer for auto scaling and high availability. And for security purpose we can use multiple services such as Cloud IAM, Cloud Identity-Aware Proxy, and Cloud Key Management Service.

Maintaining cluster health

To maintain cluster health we have to use Stackdriver Monitoring, Stackdriver Error Reporting, Stackdriver Trace, Stackdriver Debugger, and Stackdriver Logging. All these services help us in getting the exact health of the cluster and all the services.

Alpha phase is bringing data from the Data Lake into an application cluster

Depending on the source, we have to use the right GCP service. We can also use Apache Flume/Apache Storm/Apache Kafka/Apache Beam for streaming data - services from Hadoop ecosystem. Interesting things is that Apache Beam is an alternative to Cloud Data flow as well.

To ingest data from Cloud SQL, we can use the Sqoop component of Hadoop. And for batches we have plenty of options - Apache Flume can be one of those as well.

Beta phase includes cleaning of data

This phase is very internal to the Hadoop cluster and Hadoop Ecosystem, which we built using Cloud Dataproc. But we can use Apache Pig and Apache Hive to clean data. Proprietary software is also available.

From the GCP ecosystem you can use the Cloud Dataprep service - it is used for cleaning and preparing data for analysis.

Gamma phase performs transformation

As well as Hadoop tools such as Apache Pig, Spark Core, and Spark SQL - you can also use Cloud Dataflow. We can use Cloud Dataflow for batch as well as streaming data.

Delta phase graphs and reports are generated on multiple BI tools

Hadoop has very few options for graphical representation and reporting - Zeppelin is one of them. But GCP has great services such as Google Data Studio. You can integrate Google Data Studio with Cloud Dataproc for better visualization.

Code repository

All the code that we are building requires us to store the code in a repository. For this purpose, we can use GCP's Cloud Source Repository.

Services

The services that I might be using for this use case are as follows:

- Cloud Pub/Sub
- Cloud Dataflow
- Cloud Storage
- Storage Transfer Service or gsutil
- Cloud SQL
- Cloud Bigtable
- Cloud BigQuery
- Cloud Source Repository
- Cloud Dataproc
- Cloud Identity and Access Management(IAM)
- Cloud Identity-Aware Proxy
- Cloud Key Management Service
- Cloud Load Balancer
- Stackdriver Monitoring
- Stackdriver Error Reporting
- Stackdriver Trace
- Stackdriver Debugger
- Stackdriver Logging
- Cloud Dataprep
- Google Data Studio

Architecture

The high level architecture for the given use case is shown as follows:

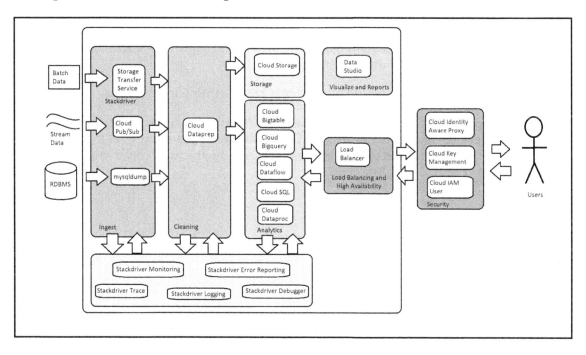

Conclusion

With this use case we can conclude that building a Data Lake is very easy and we have all the services required to build a Data Lake available in Google Cloud Platform.

Summary

In this chapter, we studied two different use cases. The first use case was related to an IoT use case and the second was for a telecom client. All three use cases have helped you in getting the complete understanding about numerous service GCP has to offer. Also you understood how they are used and at what juncture. You also learnt about all options that are available to use to perform the same tasks.

Understanding these use cases would have been a great learning to all of you.

Next up is an appendix, where I am going to explain the different services that we have in Amazon Web Services and Microsoft Azure. Once you are a bit familiar with them, we will have a side-by-side comparison of all the services offered by the three major vendors in cloud platforms.

Introduction to AWS and Azure 9

In this Appendix, we are going to learn about two prominent cloud vendors—**Amazon Web Services** (**AWS**) and **Microsoft Azure**. Firstly, I will be introducing you to AWS, and then to Azure. After having a brief overview of AWS and Azure, we will have a look at all the services that these major vendors provide.

And once you are familiar with the ecosystem of AWS and Azure, we can compare them to Google Cloud Platform (GCP)—head to head.

We will be discussing the following topics:

- Overview of AWS services
- Overview of Azure services
- Head-to-head comparison between AWS, Azure, and GCP

Amazon Web Services

We will now have a look at the primary services that AWS provides.

Compute

I am now going to explain the different services in the Compute category offered by AWS:

- **AWS EC2**: Secure and resizable virtual machines on the cloud
- **AWS EC2 Auto Scaling**: Updates compute capacity as per the requirement
- **Amazon Elastic Container Service**: Assists in running containerized applications on cloud

- **AWS Lambda**: Runs code without any infrastructure concerns you pay for compute only
- **Elastic Load Balancing**: Achieves scalability, performance, and security to make an application fault-tolerant

Storage

I am now going to explain the different services in the Storage category offered by AWS:

- **Amazon S3**: Object storage on the cloud with global reach
- **Amazon EBS**: Provides persistent block storage for virtual machines in EC2
- **Amazon EFS**: File storage on AWS—simple, scalable, and reliable
- **Amazon Glacier**: Archives your data for long-term, secure, and durable features
- **AWS Storage Gateway**: Seamless local integration to retrieve data in hybrid solutions
- **AWS Snowball**: Petabyte-scale data transport service

Database

I am now going to explain the different services in the Database category offered by AWS:

- **Amazon Aurora**: MySQL and Postgre SQL compatible databases on cloud
- **Amazon RDS**: Amazon RDS provides Amazon Aurora, Postgre SQL, MySQL, MariaDB, Oracle, and Microsoft SQL Server on cloud
- **Amazon DynamoDB**: NoSQL database with pay for throughput and storage only features
- **Amazon Redshift**: Data warehousing solution for fast, cost-effective, and simple requirements

Networking and content

I am now going to explain the different services in the Network and Content category offered by AWS:

- **Amazon VPC**: Defines your own virtual network separating it from the AWS infrastructure
- **Amazon CloudFront**: Content Delivery Network offered by AWS

- **Amazon Route53**: Route53 is the DNS solution for domain purchase
- **AWS Direct Connect**: Assists you to build a direct connection between on-premise and AWS

Developer tools

I am now going to explain the different services in the Developer Tools category offered by AWS:

- **AWS Codestar**: Builds, develops, and deploys applications on AWS
- **AWS Codecommit**: Private Git repository for securing project codes privately
- **AWS CodeBuild**: Builds and tests the code. Also test scenarios in case of high demand
- **AWS CodeDeploy**: Deploys code to various services such as EC2, AWS Lambda, and many more

Management tools

I am now going to explain the different services in the Management Tools category offered by AWS:

- **Amazon CloudWatch**: Collects and matches metrics of applications running in AWS
- **AWS Auto Scaling**: Scales your application with optimization between cost and performance
- **AWS CloudTrail**: Use it to track user activities and API usage

Machine learning

I am now going to explain the different services in the Machine Learning category offered by AWS:

- **Amazon Lex**: Builds voice and text based conversational apps that use machine learning in backend
- **Amazon Polly**: Service that converts text into speech and thus helps you to build a talking app

- **Amazon Rekognition**: Image and video analysis with the power of deep learning
- **Amazon Machine Learning**: Can create machine learning models on AWS
- **Amazon Translate**: Translates one language into another language. Simple!

Analytics

I am now going to explain the different services in the Analytics category offered by AWS:

- **Amazon Athena**: Athena is used to run SQL queries on top of S3 data
- **Amazon EMR**: Run Hadoop, Spark, HBase, and many other components on AWS
- **Amazon ElasticSearch**: Elasticsearch on the top of AWS
- **Amazon Kinesis**: Collect, process, and analyze real-time data
- **Amazon Redshift**: Provides data warehousing solutions on cloud
- **AWS Data Pipeline**: You can easily move and transform data inside AWS

Security, identity, and compliance

I am now going to explain the different services in the Security, Identity, and Compliance category offered by AWS:

- **AWS IAM**: Manages access to users and the services they access
- **Amazon Cloud Directory**: Has multiple hierarchies of data along various use cases and projects

Internet of Things

I am now going to explain the different services in the Internet of Things category offered by AWS:

- **AWS IoT Core**: Connects billions of devices to the AWS, flawlessly and easily
- **AWS IoT Analytics**: Performs analytics on the IoT devices
- **AWS IoT Button**: It can be used to connect Amazon Dash Button hardware to AWS

Migration

I am now going to explain the different services in the Migration category offered by AWS:

- **AWS Migration Hub**: Lets you track the progress of all migrations in AWS
- **AWS Server Migration Service**: Migrates on-premise servers and their workloads to AWS—securely and reliably
- **AWS Database Migration Services**: Migrates on-premises databases and their data to AWS—securely and reliably

Other services

Here we are going to discuss the other wide categories that AWS provides:

- **AR and VR**: Amazon Sumerian is the service using which you can build VR and AR applications.
- **Application** Integration: Under the Application Integration category we have services such as Amazon Simple Queue Service, Amazon Simple Notification Service, and Amazon MQ. Using these services you can work on notifications, pub/sub event based applications, mobile push, and SMS.
- **Customer Engagement**: Under the Customer Engagement category we have Amazon Connect, Amazon Pinpoint, and Amazon Simple Email Service. These services help you to maintain the customer engagement through cloud-based Contact Center, Push Notifications for mobile applications, and sending/receiving emails.
- **Business Productivity**: Alexa for Business, Amazon Chime, Amazon WorkDocs, and Amazon WorkMail are the services offered under the Business Productivity category. We can have meetings, video calls, and chats using Amazon Chime. Similarly, Amazon WorkDocs provides enterprise storage and doc sharing features, while Amazon WorkMail provides a secure email service.
- **Desktop and App Streaming**: Securely access your virtual desktop application from any device over a network and also stream desktop applications to a browser.
- **Media Services**: Media Services provides you with tools to help you build your own video content platform.
- **Mobile Services**: Helps you quickly build your mobile app and scale it.

- **Game Development**: Amazon Gamelift and Amazon Lumberyard are two different services that can help you build some great games. While Gamelift provides serves the purpose of hosting games, Lumberyard provides cross-platform 3D engines.
- **Software**: We have just one service under Software: AWS Marketplace. AWS Marketplace provides you with a single place to evaluate software and quickly find, test, buy, and deploy software.
- **Cost Management**: Services in Cost Management are built to help you access, understand, allocate, control, and optimize your AWS costs.

Overview to AWS Services

To understand different services in AWS you can refer below link.

Link: `https://www.youtube.com/watch?v=P6_8EH7xlv8`

QR code:

Microsoft Azure

We will have a look at the primary services that Azure provides.

Compute

I am now going to explain the different services in the Compute category offered by Azure:

- **Virtual machines**: Helps you to provide Linux and Windows virtual machines instantly
- **Functions**: Builds your code and submits it to Azure to let it run as serverless code
- **Linux virtual machines**: Virtual machines on cloud providing Ubuntu, RHEL, and CentoOS variants
- **SAP HANA on Azure large instances**: Deploys SAP HANA workload at a great scale
- **Windows virtual machine**: Virtual machines on cloud providing Windows, SQL Server, SharePoint, and so on

Networking

I am now going to explain the different services in the Networking category offered by Azure:

- **Content delivery network**: Makes sure content is delivered efficiently and reliably
- **Azure DNS**: DNS service by Azure
- **VPN Gateway**: To establish secure and inter-premise connections
- **Load balancer**: Used to make an application highly available in the case of any network outage
- **Virtual network**: To create your own network on the cloud

Storage

I am now going to explain the different services in the Storage category offered by Azure:

- **Storage**: Cloud storage that is scalable, durable, and highly available
- **Data Lake Store**: Build your own data lake on Azure for analytics
- **Disk Storage**: Disk storage for virtual machines - secured and persistent

- **Queue Storage**: Auto scaling in storage, as per requirement storage will go up automatically as required
- **Managed Disk**: Disk storage for virtual machines - secured and persistent
- **Blob Storage**: Object storage that is REST-based and designed for unstructured data

Web and mobile

I am now going to explain the different services in the Web and Mobile category offered by Azure:

- **App Service**: To create apps on cloud for web and mobile
- **API Management**: Helps us publish APIs to all stakeholders
- **Media Services**: Useful for encoding, storing, and streaming content in audio and video format
- **Web Apps**: Useful for deploying web apps at scale
- **Mobile Apps**: Hosts and builds databases, servers, and other components for web apps

Containers

I am now going to explain the different services in the Containers category offered by Azure:

- **Azure Container Service**: Simplified deployment, management, and operations for Kubernetes
- **Container Registry**: Helps us manage all container images

Databases

I am now going to explain the different services in the Databases category offered by Azure:

- **SQL Databases**: Managed SQL Databases
- **Azure Cosmos DB**: Globally distributed, multi-model databases
- **SQL Data Warehouse**: Enterprise-class features enabled elastic data warehouse

- **Azure Database for PostgreSQL**: Cloud-based Postgre SQL for developers
- **Azure Database for MySQL:** Cloud-based MySQL for developers
- **Azure Database Migration Service:** It is useful to migrate on-premise data to cloud.

Analytics

I am now going to explain the different services in the Analytics category offered by Azure:

- **HDInsight**: Hadoop, R, Storm, Spark, HBase - all at one place
- **Apache Storm on HDInsight**: Apache Storm on cloud
- **Apache Spark on Azure HDInsight**: Apache Spark on cloud
- **Data Factory**: Manages and orchestrates data transformation
- **Power BI**: Stunning data visualization and is fully interactive for applications

AI and machine learning

I am now going to explain the different services in the Artificial Intelligence and Machine Learning category offered by Azure:

- **Machine Learning Studio**: Builds and manages different predictive models on cloud
- **Multiple API**: Supports multiple APIs—Text Analytics, Computer Vision, Bing Search, Face, Web Language, Translator Text, Translator Speech, and many more

Internet of Things

I am now going to explain the different services in the Internet of Things category offered by Azure:

- **IoT Hub**: Builds a hub of numerous IoT devices to connect, monitor, and control
- **IoT Edge**: Passes on intelligence from cloud to IoT devices

Security and Identity

I am now going to explain the different services in the Security and Identity category offered by Azure:

- **Azure Active Directory**: Enables single sign-on for on-premise directories
- **Key Vault**: Helps you protect and safeguard security and encryption keys
- **Multi-Factor Authentication**: Provides multiple-level authentication mechanisms

Developer Tools

I am now going to explain the different services in the Developer Tools category offered by Azure:

- **Visual Studio Team Services**: Shares code, tracks work, and delivers software for teams
- **Application Insights**: Provides insights into the health of the apps

Management Tools

I am now going to explain the different services in the Management Tools category offered by Azure:

- **Backup**: Easy and reliable server data backup to the cloud
- **Scheduler**: Schedule your jobs on cloud
- **Security and Compliance**: Uses advanced cloud security to enable threat detection and prevention
- **Cloud Shell**: A browser-based shell to control Azure Cloud
- **Cost Management**: Helps you optimize all service expenses of all the services

Overview to Azure Services

To understand different services in Azure you can refer below link.

Link: https://www.youtube.com/watch?v=N0LTQDEh-2Y

QR code:

Head to head of Google Cloud Platform with Amazon Web Services and Microsoft Azure

In this section, we will learn and compare the various features of Google Cloud Platform, Amazon Web Services and Microsoft Azure.

We will compare the platforms with respect to the following parameters:

- Compute
- Storage
- Database
- Analytics and big data
- Internet of Things
- Mobile Services
- Application Services
- Networking
- Security and Identity
- Monitoring and Management

We will discuss the platforms with respect to each of these aspects, in the following sections.

Compute

The properties of these platforms according to the computing parameter are summarized in the following table:

Properties	Google Cloud Platform	Amazon Web Services	Microsoft Azure
Virtual System	Compute Engine	EC2	Virtual Machine
Autoscale	Autoscaling	Autoscaling	App Service Autoscaling
Virtual Server Disk	Persistent Disk	Elastic Blob Storage	Page Blobs
Container Management	Container Engine	EC2 Container Service	Container Service
Serverless Function	Cloud Functions	Lambda	Cloud Services
Web Applications	App Engine	Elastic Beanstalk	Web Apps
Marketplace	Cloud Launcher	AWS Marketplace	Azure Marketplace

Storage

The properties of these platforms with regard to storage are summarized in the following table:

Properties	Google Cloud Platform	Amazon Web Services	Microsoft Azure
Object	Cloud Storage	S3	Blob Storage
Archiving	Cloud Storage Nearline	Glacier and S3	Backup
Content Delivery	Cloud CDN	CloudFront	Content Delivery Network

Database

The properties of these platforms with regard to databases are summarized in the following table:

Properties	Google Cloud Platform	Amazon Web Services	Microsoft Azure
Relational Database	Cloud SQL	RDS	SQL Database
NoSQL Database	Cloud Datastore	DynamoDB	DocumentDB
Data Warehouse	BigQuery	Redshift	SQL Datawarehouse
Table Storage	Cloud Bigtable	Simple DB	Azure Redis Cache
Caching	Memcache	ElasticCache	Azure Redis Cache

Analytics and big data

The properties of these platforms according to big data analytics can be summarized to the following table:

Properties	Google Cloud Platform	Amazon Web Services	Microsoft Azure
Hadoop	Cloud Dataproc	Elastic Map Reduce	HDInsight
Data Orchestration	Cloud Dataflow	Data Pipeline	Data Factory
Analytics	Cloud Dataflow	Kinesis Analytics	Stream Analytics, Data Lake Analytics
Machine Learning	Cloud Machine Learning API	Machine Learning	Machine Learning
API	Translate, Speech, Vision	-	Language, Speech, Vision, Knowledge
Search	Search API	Elastic Search	Bing Search API
Genomics	Google Genomics	-	-

Internet of Things

The properties of these platforms with regard to IoT parameters are summarized in the following table:

Internet of Things	IoT Core	IoT	IoT Hub
Streaming Data	Cloud Dataflow, Cloud Pub/Sub	Kinesis Stream	Event Hubs

Mobile Services

The properties of these platforms with regard to mobile service parameters are summarized in the following table:

App Development	App Engine, Firebase	Mobile Hub, Cognito	Mobile Apps

Application Services

The properties of these platforms with regard to services can be summarized to the following table:

Email Service	App Engine (Email Service)	Mobile Hub, Incognito	Mobile Apps
Messaging	Cloud Pub/Sub, App Engine (Task Queue)	Simple Queue Service, Simple Notification Service	Queue Storage, Service Bus Queue
App Testing	Cloud Test Lab (front and back end)	Device (front end)	Xamarin Test Cloud (front end), Azure DevTests Labs (back end)
API Management	Cloud Endpoints	API Gateway	API Management

Networking

The properties of these platforms with regard to networking are summarized in the following table:

Networking	Cloud Virtual Network	Virtual Private Cloud	Virtual Network
DNS	Cloud DNS	Route 53	DNS Traffic Manager
Dedicated Network	Cloud Interconnect	Direct Connect	ExpressRoute
Load Balancer	Cloud Load Balancing	Elastic Load Balancing	Load Balancer

Security and Identity

The properties of these platforms with regard to security and identity are summarized in the following table:

Authentication and Authorization	Google IAM, Cloud Resource Manager, Google Identity Toolkit, Google Signin, Multi-factor Authentication	Identity and Access Management, Multi-factor Authentication	Azure AD, RBAC, Multi-factor Authentication
Encryption	Platform Level Encryption, BYOK	Key Management Services, CloudHSM, BYOK	Key Vault, BYOK
Security	Cloud Security Scanner (App Engine)	Inspector	Security Center

Monitoring and Management

The properties of these platforms with regard to monitoring and management are summarized in the following table:

Properties	Google Cloud Platform	Amazon Web Services	Microsoft Azure
Deployment Orchestration	Cloud Deployment Manager	CloudFormation, OpsWork	Automation, Resource Manager
Monitoring and Management	Cloud Console, Stackdriver, Logs API (App Engine), Cloud Mobile App, Cloud Shell	CloudWatch, CloudTrail	Log Analytics, Azure Portal, Application Insights
Optimization	Cron Service (App Engine)	Trusted Advisor	-
Source Code	Cloud Source Repositories	CodeCommit	Visual Studio Team Services
Admin	Audit Logs	Config	Azure Portal (audit logs)
Programming	Command Line Interface, Google Cloud SDK	Command Line Interface, Amazon Web Service SDK	Azure Command Line Interface, Azure PowerShell, Azure SDK

Summary

You understood many things about AWS and Azure. And later on we did a great head to head comparison of all the services that GCP has to offer.

This was the last topic of the book and we have come a long distance with respect to Cloud Analytics. We started form Cloud Computing to comparing three major cloud vendors - GCP, AWS and Azure. You should pat your back for this.

I hope you liked it.

Other Books You May Enjoy

If you enjoyed this book, you may be interested in these other books by Packt:

R Data Analysis Cookbook - Second Edition
Kuntal Ganguly

ISBN: 9781787124479

- Acquire, format and visualize your data using R
- Using R to perform an Exploratory data analysis
- Introduction to machine learning algorithms such as classification and regression
- Get started with social network analysis
- Generate dynamic reporting with Shiny
- Get started with geospatial analysis
- Handling large data with R using Spark and MongoDB
- Build Recommendation system- Collaborative Filtering, Content based and Hybrid
- Learn real world dataset examples- Fraud Detection and Image Recognition

R Data Analysis Projects
Gopi Subramanian

ISBN: 9781788621878

- Build end-to-end predictive analytics systems in R
- Build an experimental design to gather your own data and conduct analysis
- Build a recommender system from scratch using different approaches
- Use and leverage RShiny to build reactive programming applications
- Build systems for varied domains including market research, network analysis, social media analysis, and more
- Explore various R Packages such as RShiny, ggplot, recommenderlab, dplyr, and find out how to use them effectively
- Communicate modeling results using Shiny Dashboards
- Perform multi-variate time-series analysis prediction, supplemented with sensitivity analysis and risk modeling

Leave a review - let other readers know what you think

Please share your thoughts on this book with others by leaving a review on the site that you bought it from. If you purchased the book from Amazon, please leave us an honest review on this book's Amazon page. This is vital so that other potential readers can see and use your unbiased opinion to make purchasing decisions, we can understand what our customers think about our products, and our authors can see your feedback on the title that they have worked with Packt to create. It will only take a few minutes of your time, but is valuable to other potential customers, our authors, and Packt. Thank you!

Index

V

virtual machine (VM) 6
Virtual Private Cloud (VPC) 68
virtualization 52
Vision API
  about 88

URL 89

W

web mining recommendation
  with TensorFlow 218
World Wide Web 218

CPSIA information can be obtained
at www.ICGtesting.com
Printed in the USA
BVOW11s0813230418
514169BV00023B/1249/P

9 781788 839686